M000208084

Kristel Ward has written a great devotional! Not only is she an excellent writer and storyteller but she also pulls out truths from God's Word that will help you as you navigate this day with courage and strength. Enjoy every page!

Holly Wagner | founding pastor, Oasis Church; founder, She Rises; author, *Find Your Brave*

Kristel carries a message this generation desperately needs. She pulls from her own powerful story of overcoming and uncovers biblical truth to help us remain emotionally and mentally healthy in even the darkest of times. It's been a joy to run alongside her in the Truth Academy, and I can't wait for this devotional to get out into the world.

Havilah Cunnington | founder, Truth to Table

Kristel Ward's new book, *Grace to Grow*, speaks straight to the heart. It beautifully calms negative voices and internal doubts that make us feel like we are not enough or that we lack what is needed to win. Each devotion is written in a way that encourages readers to expect good things for their future. This positive, energetic, and hope-filled read is hard to put down.

Tracey Mitchell | TV host; author, *Becoming Brave*

When the *what if* questions disrupt your peace, *Grace to Grow* is the place to go. Kristel Ward ever so gently guides you back to quieting the chaos and growing closer to Jesus, our true peace. Overcome your anxiety and find your way to a calm heart by studying this beautifully written, biblically based devotional.

Alita Reynolds | president, Women of Faith

This devotional is everything! Kristel shares real experiences that will help you understand God's grace and inspire you to grow closer to him. Listen, you need to get yourself a copy. You can thank me later.

Valencia Maseko-Khumalo | founder, Let's Grow Sisters

Kristel's open, honest, and practical writing style speaks to the heart. Her life and ministry have touched me personally, and I know you will be refreshed as you allow her devotions to encourage you.

Billie Hunt | author; founder, Billie Hunt Ministries

GRACE

to

GROW

40
Devotions to
Release Anxiety and
Dive into Purpose

KRISTEL WARD

BroadStreet
P U B L I S H I N G

BroadStreet Publishing® Group, LLC
Savage, Minnesota, USA
BroadStreetPublishing.com

Grace to Grow: 40 Devotions to Release Anxiety and Dive into Purpose
Copyright © 2022 Kristel Ward

9781424564514 (faux leather)
9781424564521 (ebook)

All rights reserved. No part of this book may be reproduced in any form, except for brief quotations in printed reviews, without permission in writing from the publisher.

Scripture quotations marked TPT are from The Passion Translation®. Copyright © 2017, 2018, 2020 by Passion & Fire Ministries, Inc. Used by permission. All rights reserved. ThePassionTranslation.com. Scripture quotations marked NKJV are taken from the New King James Version®. Copyright © 1982 by Thomas Nelson. Used by permission. All rights reserved. Scripture quotations marked NLT are taken from the Holy Bible, New Living Translation, copyright © 1996, 2004, 2015 by Tyndale House Foundation. Used by permission of Tyndale House Publishers, a Division of Tyndale House Ministries, Carol Stream, Illinois 60188. All rights reserved. Scripture quotations marked NIV are taken from The Holy Bible, New International Version® NIV®. Copyright © 1973, 1978, 1984, 2011 by Biblica, Inc.™ Used by permission. All rights reserved worldwide. Scripture quotations marked ESV are taken from the ESV® Bible (The Holy Bible, English Standard Version®), copyright © 2001 by Crossway, a publishing ministry of Good News Publishers. Used by permission. All rights reserved. Scripture quotations marked MSG are taken from THE MESSAGE, copyright © 1993, 2002, 2018 by Eugene H. Peterson. Used by permission of NavPress. All rights reserved. Represented by Tyndale House Publishers, a Division of Tyndale House Ministries. Scripture quotations marked NCV are taken from the New Century Version®. Copyright © 2005 by Thomas Nelson. Used by permission. All rights reserved. Quoted by permission. All rights reserved. Scripture quotations marked AMP are taken from the Amplified® Bible (AMP). Copyright © 2015 by The Lockman Foundation. Used by permission. www.Lockman.org.

Stock or custom editions of BroadStreet Publishing titles may be purchased in bulk for educational, business, ministry, fundraising, or sales promotional use. For information, please email orders@broadstreetpublishing.com.

Agent: Tracey Mitchell, tracy@tracymitchell.com

Cover and interior by Garborg Design at GarborgDesign.com

Printed in China

22 23 24 25 26 5 4 3 2 1

Dedication

To Mom. Thank you for being my biggest fan
and for your unconditional love.

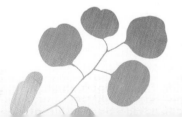

Contents

Introduction

Anxiety is armed with the weighty question of *what if? What if I fail? What if I choose wrongly?* But *what if* the worries of tomorrow can be washed away? *Grace to Grow* will help you to disarm anxiety by stripping away its power. As you lean into grace, you will be surprised by the level of confidence, clarity, and security that flows your way. A thriving relationship with God is not an impossibility but an invitation into adventure. In these pages, you will discover how to

- accept God's invitation to intimacy,
- bring overwhelming situations into focus,
- receive hope for tomorrow,
- transform stormy seasons into times of spiritual growth, and
- rest in God's grace.

Peace is possible. My prayer is that this devotional will help you rise above the chaos and embrace grace today. Each devotion delivers insight to propel you forward in your purpose. The result is a lifestyle free from fear and flooded with grace.

With love,
Kristel Ward

The Storm

"*I remember the old man who said
he had had a great many troubles in his life,
but the worst of them never happened.*"
PRESIDENT JAMES A. GARFIELD

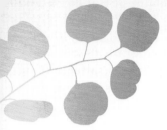

Faith Is Rising

Faith comes by hearing,
and hearing by the word of God.
ROMANS 10:17 NKJV

Abbey and Emma announced, "Evan's awake!" as they twirled into the nursery. I stumbled behind with coffee in hand. My four-month-old son flashed the cheeser grin that I liked to call *Mr. Wonderful.* As we cooed back, his happy face faded. Evan's eyes glazed over, shifted to the side, and rolled backward. His limbs drew in tightly as his tiny body began jerking in convulsions. "Hurry, get my phone," I said to Abbey. Shaking hands made it difficult for my fingers to find 911.

A steady male voice met me on the other end of the line. "911 emergency response, what's your emergency?"

"My son is having a seizure! His face is turning blue!" I fought to keep control when I wanted to scream in terror. Quick calming questions came through the phone as the operator kept me talking. Evan's clenched fists finally released as his body began to relax. The three-minute seizure felt like an eternity. I grabbed my baby and clutched him to my chest as we watched the ambulance arrive from the nursery window.

I wish I could say that was the worst day of my life, but that one day stretched into thirty. Evan continued to seize when waking from sleep. In the mornings, during naps, and at night, the seizures kept coming. The atmosphere of our home became tense and pressurized. I grasped for hope, strength, and sanity. In one month, Evan had more than seventy seizures. I felt like I might lose my mind and possibly my marriage.

One Sunday, Evan and I were alone while my husband, BJ, and the girls went to church. Worship music played on repeat as a constant prayer in my heart. Evan had fallen asleep in my lap, and I was afraid to move and potentially wake him. As he drifted out of his sleep, I recognized the signs of another seizure. I wanted to cry. Scream. Mourn. As the song played through the air, I grasped for one more straw of strength. And I worshiped. While holding my son's seizing body I raised heavy hands in honor to the Lord. I lifted my voice and sang to him with the last bit of courage I could find. My song rang out, "Emmanuel, you're God with me. My Comforter, very present help when eyes can't see." The Lord responded to my fragile cry. In my lowest moment God's presence washed over my shattered heart.

It wasn't long after this worshiping that the gentle words of God resonated within me. *Your son is going to be fine*. Encouragement swept through my soul. I gripped onto that promise like a life preserver. When fear fractured my thoughts, I declared to myself, *No, my son is going to be fine*. I pulled truth from Scripture and prayed it over my family. The healing of my traumatized mind came in stages. Daily practices of choosing worship over worry, praise over powerlessness, and promises over lies kept me moving forward. Faith developed within as God demonstrated his faithfulness.

I couldn't listen to that worship song again for years, but it plays on repeat today while I write these words to you. As the familiar melody spills from my phone, I sense the same presence of God washing over me that appeared in that moment of desperation. When fear whispers false promises over my son, I still cling to the words the Lord spoke long ago. That tiny baby is now an active kid. He drives me crazy asking one million questions. Evan has been seizure-free for many years. God's presence and promises still hold me firm on days when my thoughts are unsettled.

If anxiety comes calling today, I encourage you to lift up words of worship to God. Consider declaring truth from Scripture out loud over your situation. Not sure where to find a verse? Just google it. Listen for the Lord's gentle encouragement. His peace confronts the chaos. Anxiety is not God's answer for you, friend. Faith is rising today.

Pause to Reflect

- When fear strikes, counter back by proclaiming God's goodness.
- Redirect anxious thoughts to the truth of Scripture.
- Faith is promoted by applying God's promises.

Pause to Pray

Lord, when anxiety invades my thoughts, help me cling to your words. I ask you to speak encouragement to my heart. I believe that the promises of Scripture are for me. Father, fear is a liar, and I want no part of it. Increase my faith as I trust in you. In Jesus' name. Amen.

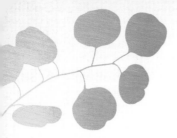

Save Me

I called on the name of the LORD:
"Please, LORD, save me!"
How kind the LORD is!
How good he is!
So merciful, this God of ours!
PSALM 116:4–5 NLT

I imagine the wind sent chills down the spines of the sailors. The storm tortured the ship with waves, as streaks of light cut across the sky. Although they had been pulling the oars all night, the men weren't much closer to their destination. Their minds and muscles fatigued to the point of failure. Sinking in the middle of the sea seemed inevitable.

One of the men shouted, "We're going to have to let her run aground."

Peter responded over the other twelve between rows, "No, that's too risky."

The rest of the disciples held their paddles as rain poured over their faces. "What do you want us to do then?"

"I...I..." Peter dropped his head and oars too.

As the crew looked out over the water, a figure approached the ship. The disciples couldn't identify it through the wind, but it was coming closer. The men gripped the railing. "It's...it's a ghost!"

Jesus stopped his forward motion. "Don't fear! Have courage!" The command bounced off the men as they blinked in disbelief. Jesus looked at each disciple and weighed his next words. "I AM."

The declaration motivated Peter to move. "Lord, if it is you, command me to come to you on the water" (Matthew 14:28 ESV).

The disciples grabbed at Peter as he swung his legs over the side of the ship. "What are you doing?" Peter swatted their reaches and braced himself on the side of the boat. With eyes shut, he threw himself over the ledge. He waited for the water to submerge him. It didn't. Everyone held their breath, including Jesus. The waves rolled beneath Peter's feet but somehow stayed firm. He slid one foot forward. Then another. Peter locked on Jesus as he shuffled closer.

Suddenly the water rushed beneath him as the wind picked up. Peter watched as the waves crested, then he turned back to Jesus. His feet sank into the water as panic pulled him under. Peter was stuck between the storm and the savior. "'Save me, Lord!' he shouted" (v. 30 NLT). Jesus immediately grabbed Peter's hand and pulled him up.

Jesus' grip held Peter firm until he relaxed. "Why is your faith so weak?" Jesus sighed and walked Peter back to the boat, as the other disciples stood against the wind and stared. "Can one of you help us up?" With Jesus aboard, the storm went silent. When the disciples looked ahead, the boat was resting onshore. The reality of their rescue washed over them, and each man dropped to his knees. "You really are the Son of God!" (v. 33 NLT).

When waves of worry, doubt, and stress threaten to drown you, reach out to Jesus. Call out your own *Save me!* to the Lord. In that two-word phrase is a distress signal for total rescue. In Greek, it is *sōzō*, which is to "save, deliver, and protect." The Lord embraces all who call on him.

Jesus is the I AM who empowers you to do what seems impossible. He is the Savior who reaches down to pull you up. Jesus is Emmanuel, the *God-with-you*. He climbs into your life and calms the storm. Jesus is the deliverer who directs you to the destination. He is the author of time who can multiply it to meet life's demands. Jesus is the source of all your needs, and waves of chaos still obey him.

Pause to Reflect

- When life overwhelms and underdelivers, call out *Save Me*! to the Lord.
- Jesus has all power, is with you, and cares about every problem.
- Winds of worry and waves of stress must bow to the King of kings.

Pause to Pray

Lord Jesus, you're all I need when I feel like I'm sinking. Today, I call out to you to save me from the storms. Deliver me from sin. Rescue me from trouble. Protect me from harm. All the waves in my life must submit to you. You are the great I AM, and you're with me. In Jesus' name. Amen.

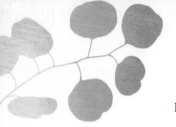

Fireproof

When you walk through fire you shall not be burned, and the flame shall not consume you. For I am the LORD your God, the Holy One of Israel, your Savior.
ISAIAH 43:2–3 ESV

I can't believe I'm about to tell you this story. It was not a bright moment in our marriage.

BJ and I once went an entire year without going on a date. Not a single date. And no, it's not because of kids or lack of money, though I'd love for you to think that. I was pregnant with our first baby. We both started new jobs. I was consumed with excelling in my new teaching career. BJ plunged himself into limitless overtime as he assumed the role of provider for our growing family. We both slaved over our stresses. When Abbey was born, adding a baby compounded the problems. My overachiever issues and his provider complex didn't clash in conflict but peeled us apart in silence.

At work one day, a coworker's surprise flowers from her spouse poked at my hidden heartache. At home that evening, BJ and I discussed the issues that were nonchalantly suffocating our marriage. I struggled with defining my emotions. "I…I just feel like you don't love me. I mean, I know you do, but…"

BJ looked as if my statement slapped his face. "I don't understand how you could think that. I've been working so hard *because* I love you. Both of you."

"But, babe, when was the last time we even went on a date?" We stared at each other as we mentally flipped the calendar to our previous night out. The shock must have shown in my expression. "I think it was the month before I got pregnant with Abbey." We looked down at our two-month-old daughter in my lap.

BJ's head dropped to his hands. "I'm so sorry. I guess I just…I got caught up in saving money now that we have a baby. We'll fix it."

We stepped into the movie theater heavyhearted but hand in hand. The film that night was *Fireproof*, which was set on a failing marriage. How fitting. The lead character, Caleb, was a firefighter who was addicted to pornography. His wife, Catherine, was wounded and bitter over his betrayal. Their relationship rifted from neglect. With divorce papers in hand, Caleb remembered the fundamental statement of his firehouse: *Never leave your partner behind.*[1] He smashed his porn-filled computer with a baseball bat and left roses for Catherine in its place. He buried his face daily in prayer for their marriage. In the end, they remembered why they fell in love in the first place. The final scene ended with a longing kiss of restoration.

I was approaching hot-mess status as the lights flipped on in the theater. Postpartum hormones and stories too close to home had me flirting with the edge of my emotions. By the time we reached the lobby, I lost it. All of it. Months of pent-up pain, doubts, and questions poured out in full-on sobs. The kind of cry that was coupled with gasps for breath between wails. I buried myself in my husband's chest in an attempt to hide from onlookers. None of them were brave enough to ask. My mortifying movie theater meltdown was a continual reminder to safeguard my marriage.

The absurdity of my reaction is funny now but not in the moment. It came at the tail end of a terrible year for BJ and me. Yet I looked back and saw how God steadied us in uncertain times. Neglect could have destroyed our marriage. It didn't. God used the struggle to gently correct our ignorance. More than a decade later we are stronger. After walking through many difficulties together, our marriage is more intimate. God never left us in the fire.

You may be facing blazing battles today. You may feel overwhelmed and underprepared, but please know you are never forsaken. When the flames get high, allow God's soothing presence to surround you. God is with you in the furnace (Daniel 3:25). The fire never gets too hot for him.

Pause to Reflect

- Turn to God when you feel physically exhausted and emotionally expended.
- The Lord is with you in every trying circumstance.
- Walking through fiery trials with God deepens intimacy with him.

Pause to Pray

Lord Holy Spirit, when the battle feels hot and the flames are closing in, I cling to you. I know you never leave me in the fire. Please circle me with your life-giving presence. You're always near, and your heart is to help. I trust you. In Jesus' name I pray. Amen.

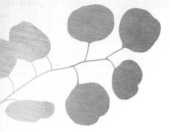

Put on Praise

"The Spirit of the Lord GOD is upon Me…To console
those who mourn in Zion, To give them beauty for
ashes, The oil of joy for mourning, The garment of
praise for the spirit of heaviness; That they may be
called trees of righteousness, The planting of the LORD,
that He may be glorified."

ISAIAH 61:1, 3 NKJV

Preteen me sat on a burnt orange pew with my arms
crossed, while clapping echoed over the crowd. My
mom had made me start coming to church months
before, and I was determined to express my dissat-
isfaction. I glanced around the sanctuary watching
bodies sway while singing. A thin, middle-aged
woman caught my attention in the front corner of the
room. Long brown curls down the back of her dress
bounced to another beat. The rest of us didn't exist as
she snapped her fingers and kicked up her heels. This
lady seemed to share a secret with God.

The jubilant dancer was Miss Joy. She could be found in the same front row section every Sunday. I discovered Miss Joy had received a terminal diagnosis only a few months prior. She certainly knew something I didn't. This lady danced in a failing body while I sat motionless in excellent health. Over the next year I watched as Miss Joy kicked up the carpet in her little corner of the church. As her frame was slowing, mine seemed to be moving more. Before long I was singing and swaying along. Years after Miss Joy's spot was empty, an older me filled it with my own praise to God. Miss Joy never knew it, but she shared her secret with me.

Praise is a celebration of the goodness of God. It may not always look like dancing or singing, but it always proclaims God's glorious character. Praise places God on the throne of our minds. Our adoration is not dependent on the situations surrounding us. When the world is falling apart, God is still worthy of honor. Miss Joy understood that God is good regardless of circumstances. Our life on earth is temporary, but God's loving-kindness is eternal. These moments with the Lord aren't always experienced from Sunday sanctuaries. Sometimes they are made of broken prayers lifted from ordinary places.

I recently listened to a world-renowned worship leader share the story of her most successful song. It has been sung weekly by over thirty million people worldwide, though the song is nearly thirty years old.[2] The notes were not written in a collaboration session with multiple musicians. No, she tapped at an old piano in her kids' playroom. The lyrics didn't fall into place in her peaceful morning prayer time. She wrote on a stressful day when bills were mounting high, money was low, and kids were everywhere. That song has been translated into over twenty languages and sung for a pope at the Vatican and for an American president.[3]

Praise is higher than any lyric on a screen. It can be set to music or to the sway of a rocking chair. It can happen in a church, in our car, at an old piano, and in a crisis. As we put on praise like a garment, we shake off the shackles of despair. Hope rises in our hearts as we remember the greatness of God.

If you're feeling weighted with weariness today, consider praising God. An upbeat worship song or even an old familiar hymn might help. It may feel like a stark contrast to your emotions at first. As you declare who God is over the difficulties, I believe the discouragement will lift. Praise may not change the circumstances, but it puts problems in perspective next to a mighty God.

Pause to Reflect

- Praise declares God's greatness beyond the trials.
- In good times and bad, God is still worthy of adoration.
- As we lift praise to the Lord, heaviness falls off our shoulders.

Pause to Pray

Lord, you are good and only do good. Great is your faithfulness. You clothe me with strength for today and wisdom for tomorrow. Your loving-kindness is better than life itself. Even in the darkest night, you are close beside me. I praise you today because you are beyond worthy. In Jesus' name I pray. Amen.

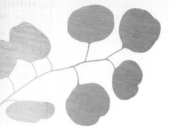

Swing Back

> "In that coming day no weapon turned against you will succeed. You will silence every voice raised up to accuse you. These benefits are enjoyed by the servants of the Lord; their vindication will come from me. I, the Lord, have spoken!"
>
> Isaiah 54:17 NLT

Johnny walked into the gym head down. Threats from guys at work pushed him into training. Soon he was paired up with Roger, a middle-aged coach who seemed a bit round and short for boxing. While Roger introduced some basics in the ring, another figure caught Johnny's attention. In the gym corner was a man pounding on the heavy bag as if he might break it open. The word *FRIDGE* was written across his shorts in fat letters. A chill went down Johnny's spine as Roger brought his attention back to the punching mitts. The distraction continued for weeks. Fridge would punish the bag and derail Johnny's focus from his coach.

At the end of a training session, Coach Roger suited up and called Fridge into the ring. Johnny slid through the ropes and braced to witness a beatdown. Coach Roger tucked his chin to his chest, raised his gloves, and shuffled toward the opponent. Fridge reared back for a punch. Before the fist could land, Roger countered with a left hook. Stunned, Fridge stepped back and shook it off. Again he lunged forward for a blow. Coach Roger ducked and countered with two straight punches. Now Fridge's nose was bleeding. He came back with flailing gloves toward Roger. Each time Coach dodged and countered with a combination. The bell sounded. Fridge threw down his gear, ducked through the ropes, and walked out. Johnny saw a beatdown, but it was Roger who dealt it. No one saw Fridge in the gym again.[4]

Sometimes life feels like flying gloves to the face. It can seem as if troubles come at us in a fury. Then we have an enemy who wants to compound the issues. Satan likes to use problems as an attempt to render us powerless. He jabs with lies, uppercuts with accusations, and rains down with condemnation. Satan would love for us to think that he's the king of the ring, but he's hiding a secret. He has already lost. Satan was stripped of power when Jesus died on the cross. Now he wails at us, attempting to regain his title. The experienced fighter doesn't just take Satan's shots. No, he knows how to use Satan's blows against him.

Times can be tough, but so are you. When Satan takes his swings, pop him back in the mouth with the Word of God. Grab a Scripture verse on your situation and hurl it his way. When he strikes with fear over your finances, hit back with *my God shall supply all my needs according to his riches and glory* (Philippians 4:19). Declare those words out loud over your family. When he attacks with anxiety over the future, right-hook him with *my God knows the plans he has for me* (Jeremiah 29:11). Speak that Scripture verse over yourself. When he counters with accusations to your conscience, uppercut him with *there is no condemnation for those who are in Christ Jesus* (Romans 8:1). Say it back at him. No weapon in his arsenal will win as you counter his attacks with the Word of God (Isaiah 54:17).

The Philly Shell is a defensive boxing stance that packs an offensive punch. The fighter stands slightly offset to the opponent with his backhand curled up to his face and his leading glove near his chest. As the challenger takes a shot, the Philly Shell boxer glances it off his shoulder. Now the enemy is off-balance. He counters the missed blow with a wrecking right hook. When employed correctly, the challenger is found flat on his back. Knockout. Floyd "Money" Mayweather made the Philly Shell famous by executing it with precision. At the end of his career Mayweather retired

50–0. He was one of a small, elite class of boxers to remain undefeated.[5]

A storm of shots may be coming against you, but don't let life pin you against the ropes. Shrug struggles off the shoulder and hit back with promises in Scripture. Jesus has all power, authority, and victory, and he lives in you.

Pause to Reflect

- When problems punch at you, don't back down in defeat.
- Satan is an enemy who attempts to render Christians powerless.
- Swing back at Satan's lies with Scripture.

Pause to Pray

Heavenly Father, when life comes against me, I have the power of your Word. You already defeated Satan by the cross. Help me silence every lie with the truth of Scripture. Thank you, Lord, that I am victorious in you. In Jesus' name I pray. Amen.

The Grace

"Grace is never cheap. It is absolutely free to us,
but infinitely expensive to God."[6]
JERRY BRIDGES

Grace Lifts

Praise God our savior!
For each day he carries us in his arms.
PSALM 68:19 NLT

I began my professional career as a tenth-grade
World History teacher in some of the toughest schools
in Texas. Gang activity and riots were common occur-
rences. In my third year, my task was to help launch
a virtual high school. This was during a time when
online learning was beginning. We had to design the
courses ourselves because we had a limited operating
budget. I was also pregnant with my first baby and
starting a staff position at church. Stress seared my
mind as I felt stretched beyond my limits.

Abbey was born five weeks before school started.
My course was incomplete, and I dreaded leaving my
baby for work. Abbey stayed with my parents during
the first week of school because she was too young for

daycare. Mom-guilt, work stress, and life pressures seemed suffocating.

In those days, life looked dark, but there were signs of growth beneath the surface. Because I was teaching online, I was able to work from home three days per week. One hundred percent of my students passed the state exams by my third year at that school. I used the skills I learned as a teacher to help launch churches, lead teams, and write Bible curriculum. If possible, I would tell my younger self, *Relax. God's grace carries you.*

A sign hangs on our wall at home that reads, "The will of God will never take you where the grace of God will not protect you." It was a gift from one of the founders of our church, Bishop Jimmy Davidson, who was also a source of inspiration for my writing career. One day, Bishop pointed his finger at me and said, "I want a book outline by next week."

I responded, "Well, I guess I better go pray then." Bishop encouraged me to follow God's path for my life and supported me along the way.

Not long after this conversation, Bishop preached a sermon titled "Grace Lifts Me." It was based on a verse from John 15: "Every branch in Me that does not bear fruit He takes away" (John 15:2 NKJV). This passage seems harsh, but a hidden treasure lies within it. The phrase *He takes away* in Greek

also means "to lift up." God is not a cruel taskmaster but a gentle gardener who cares for the vines.

A trip to a vineyard inspired Bishop's sermon. A vinedresser came by as Bishop stood in seemingly endless rows of grapevines. The vinedresser stepped back, stared at one of the plants, then knelt in the dirt. He said, "The vine is healthy, but this branch is not fruiting. Mud creates a coating that prevents it from absorbing sunlight. It has the capacity to produce a crop, but the debris is blocking the necessary nutrients." The vinedresser lifted the branch, washed it, and attached it to the supporting wire. It's easy to see that, in the same way, God's grace lovingly lifts us. It cleanses off the heaviness of life and gently secures us back to the Lord, our Vine.

I was present with Bishop the day he passed away. The following week, I was scheduled to speak to our congregation. In his honor, I shared his sermon, "Grace Lifts Me."

In the film *A Good Year*, a wealthy stockbroker moves to the French wine country. Henry, the stockbroker, is set to inherit his uncle's vineyard, but experts had labeled the vines as worthless. Henry fusses with the difficult vinedresser, or *vigneron* in French, because of his strange methods. One day he sees the vigneron singing over the vines. When Henry asks why he does such an odd thing, the Frenchman explains, "My whole life, people laughed at me for singing to the vines. I explained that, someday, the vines would sing back."[7] In the end, Henry learns that the worthless vines had been producing a private label of exquisite wine all along.

The Lord is singing over you today. Grace carries you just as it steadied me during my teaching career. God cleanses the mud that life throws your way. The Holy Spirit helps keep you connected to the Lord and produces extraordinary fruit from your life. Grace is immeasurable, fully available, and unfailing. Allow grace to lift you today.

Pause to Reflect

- Grace carries you in tough times.
- God is not a harsh taskmaster but a loving gardener.
- When life leaves marks on you, grace cleanses and restores you to the source of strength.

Pause to Pray

Lord, I surrender to grace today. When harsh environments weigh me down, I ask you to wash me and keep me connected to you. In Jesus' name I pray. Amen.

Barely-Making-It Mode

*So let us come boldly to the throne of our gracious God.
There we will receive his mercy, and we will find grace
to help us when we need it most.*
HEBREWS 4:16 NLT

George Mallory was absentminded. He once forgot his pipe on the ledge of a mountain and made a near-impossible climb to retrieve it.[8] At thirty-seven years old, he set out to be the first person to scale Mount Everest, the highest point on earth. Everest's ominous peak towers over twenty-nine-thousand feet above sea level and borders Nepal and Tibet. In 1924, Mallory and his climbing partner, Andrew Irvine, broke camp to claw their way to the top. Mallory kept a picture of his wife, Ruth, in his pocket and promised to plant the photograph on the peak.[9] To reach his goal, he strapped a new invention, an odd-shaped oxygen tube, on his back. The local tribesman mocked the strange cylinders and called them "English Air."[10]

The primitive oxygen tanks were faulty and weighed over thirty-three pounds each.[11] At least two tubes per person were needed for a successful climb. Mallory brought along the young engineering expert, Irvine, to fix any potential oxygen-related problems.

The tanks arrived damaged. Apparently, the engineering company did not follow Irvine's guidelines. He wrote home before leaving basecamp, "The oxygen tank has already been boggled…breaks if you touch it."[12] They set out to conquer Everest despite the damaged equipment.

On June 8, 1924, another climber spotted Mallory and Irvine making a strong ascent about eight hundred feet from the summit.[13] As they disappeared behind the mountain mist, that was the last time anyone saw Mallory and Irvine alive.

Nearly thirty years later, Edmund Hillary and Tenzing Norgay were the first to plant their frozen boots on the top of the world. Armed with a specially designed oxygen breathing apparatus, the two mounted the summit of Everest on May 29, 1953.[14] Within minutes of their ascension, they scoured the peak for signs of Mallory and Irvine. They found nothing.

George Mallory's body was discovered seventy-five years after he mysteriously vanished.[15] All of his belongings were intact, preserved by the snow. Yet, his camera and the picture of his wife were missing.[16] Irvine's body was never found. No conclusive evidence has been discovered to prove whether the two were the first to reach the summit of Everest. The world may never know. Mallory never lived to tell the story. Thirty years passed until another group accomplished what George set out to do. The outcome may have been different had Mallory had proper oxygen tanks.

God's grace is the oxygen tank that enables us to scale personal mountains. Many of us are living with the breath knocked out of us. We have set up basecamp in the land of *barely-making-it*. Grace gives access to abundant life. It is the mask by which we receive encouragement from the Holy Spirit. We can do great things with God when armed with grace.

There have been times when the mountain in front of me looked unscalable. Life has left me breathless, hopeless, and barely surviving. Simple tasks consumed my energy and left little for creative ability. My dreams felt dormant. I have come to realize that God did not design his children to dwell in survival mode. His grace is sufficient to thrive in every circumstance.

If you're stuck in *barely-making-it* today, I encourage you to trust God for grace. Believe in faith that grace is more than enough for whatever you need. You will find it in generous supply in God's presence. As you connect with him in prayer, his goodness gives you strength. Take a deep breath and climb forward. Strap on grace and scale mountains today.

Pause to Reflect

- God's children are made to dwell in abundance, not mundane existence.
- Grace gives access to the encouragement of the Holy Spirit.
- God's grace is sufficient to carry us through difficult circumstances.

Pause to Pray

Father, I receive your grace today. I don't want to live in survival mode but to thrive in abundant life. Grace is more than enough for me in every situation. In Jesus' name I pray. Amen.

Embrace Grace

He answered me, "My grace is always more than enough for you, and my power finds its full expression through your weakness." So I will celebrate my weaknesses, for when I'm weak I sense more deeply the mighty power of Christ living in me.

2 CORINTHIANS 12:9–10 TPT

Rory's mom died yesterday. We don't know the circumstances surrounding her death yet." Justine Jenkin fought back her emotions as our kids ran circles around the dining room table. After another cup of coffee Justine finally got to the point. "The State wants us to adopt Rory."

I took a moment to let those words sink in. "What do you guys think about that? It's a big step. You are already busy with three kids." Both Justine and Jeff were great parents, but this was a lot even for them to take on.

"Yeah, really big. But we've talked about it and prayed together, and we want to do it." Her voice quivered, but I could see resolution in her eyes.

"Would you continue to foster then?" I didn't want my words to go against her convictions, but I felt the situation was a little overwhelming. Or maybe it was the Nerf gun war happening under the table that made me feel unsettled.

"That was a tough one." Justine fumbled with her empty coffee mug. "Kids need foster parents because they don't have anyone else. If we have to go through some tough times to support them…well, yes." Then she remembered another piece of the story. "Oh, and um…," she choked on the words, unsure if she wanted to share them. With a deep breath she decided to let them go. "Well, I'm pregnant."

"Oh, honey!" I blurted. We both stared at each other a second before our shock rolled over into laughter. "Well, okay then."

Justine juggled four kids, managed her first-trimester pregnancy, and handled Rory's adoption case. I couldn't help but notice the sense of peace that she seemed to experience. With a baby on her hip and another bulging out her belly, she brought her family to church, attended small group meetings, and met her husband for lunch most days. During this time, Rory went back and forth between his biological extended family and Justine and Jeff. When things finally settled,

Rory went to live with and be adopted by a loving family who already had his sister. The Jenkins were able to share holidays and birthdays with Rory regularly. Oh, and Justine's fourth baby? Her name is Grace.

The extravagant grace of God is beyond imagination. It hovers over us from the moment we say our first prayer and every day forward. Grace is the most remarkable in our weakest moments. We might not all become foster parents like Justine, but none of us is immune to experiencing overwhelming situations.

Life can try to jerk away your joy with a ping of a text message. Laundry spills over the basket while dishes overflow the sink. The kids scream as Nerf bullets blaze overhead. When struggles demand attention like a defiant toddler, take a deep breath, and receive grace. It is sufficient for you. If strength is faltering and emotions are frayed, reach out and take grace by the hand. Grace empowers you when life engulfs you. Rest in God's generous grace today.

Pause to Reflect

- Grace is constant and steady when life feels chaotic and uneasy.

- Rest and know that our Father never forsakes his children and that his mercy never fails.

- Grace empowers you to stand strong in seemingly impossible situations.

Pause to Pray

Heavenly Father, you are my provider and protector in time of need. You never abandon me, and you richly supply all my needs. I rest in you today. Your grace is more than enough. In Jesus' name. Amen.

The Invitation

*For all this was lavished upon us through the rich
experience of knowing him who has called us by name
and invited us to come to him through a glorious
manifestation of his goodness.*

2 PETER 1:3 TPT

I imagined that the world spun through tears as
angry hands dragged her through the town square.
Resisting was pointless. There was proof this time.
No matter how hard she fought, the same patterns of
behavior kept sucking her back in. She had brushed
away his glances for days. "Go home to your wife," she
scolded, but he only moved closer.

"No, she's not like you. It was just a family
arrangement," he whispered. It wasn't that the woman
wanted to give in, but the will to fight slipped through
her fingers like sand. She began to think, *Maybe this is
just who I am?* Hanging her head, she let him into her
home.

43

Within minutes her bedroom was filled with enraged voices. Men in dark apparel attacked her. It took her a moment to sort out that they were local priests. They screamed for her to get up and dress herself. She questioned, *How did they...?* The woman shot eyes back at her pursuer in the bed as the rabbis tore her from the house.

Before long, her face hit the ground at the feet of another rabbi and an angry crowd. "Teacher...this woman was caught in the act of adultery. The law of Moses says to stone her. What do you say?" (John 8:4–5 NLT). The Pharisees demanded a verdict. Shame crept over like a shadow as they exposed her secret sins. The rabbi met the mob's chants with silence. Slowly the woman lifted her head and watched as the rabbi, Jesus, knelt and began to write in the dirt.

After a long hush, Jesus responded. "Okay"— the woman wilted into the sand—"whichever one of you has not sinned, step forward and throw the first stone." She braced herself for the impact of the rocks, but to her amazement, no one moved. She watched as each Pharisee dropped his stone and walked away. Jesus reached to her and said, "Where are your accusers? Didn't even one of them condemn you?" (v. 10 NLT). The woman recognized that her trial was over before it began.

She responded, "No, Lord."

The next words erased her self-accusations: "Neither do I condemn you; go, and from now on sin no more" (v. 11 ESV). She wiped her tear-stained face and stumbled to get up. Turning to head home, the woman marveled at the hope rising in her heart. Hope for a fresh start.

Jesus extended grace when everyone else wanted to sling stones. Capital punishment for adultery was rarely carried out because two or more reliable witnesses had to see the sexual act occur. Their stories had to match precisely. Furthermore, where was the adulterer in the trial? The same law in Leviticus 20:10 that condemned the woman applied to the man as well. The woman's story was most likely more about the priests plotting to discredit Jesus than to condemn her for adultery. There were apparent holes in the case against her, but the burden of proof was firmly met. She had been caught in the act.

The slamming gavel of judgment didn't bring the woman healing. It was the gentle gift of grace that lifted her from the ground. However, Jesus didn't excuse or ignore her guilt. He closed the conversation by commanding her to sin no more. Grace isn't a license to sin. Yet Scripture is clear that when we sin, Jesus is our Advocate. First John 1:9 (NKJV) lays out an avenue of access to grace: "If we confess our sins, He is faithful and just to forgive us our sins and to cleanse us from all unrighteousness." We all fall short of God's glory, but forgiveness flows through Jesus.

The past is not powerful enough to disqualify us from the grace of God. Throughout the Scriptures, God turns murderers into missionaries, worriers into warriors, and victims into victors. He specializes in redeeming impossible situations. Despite every failure and flaw, we have an invitation to an intimate relationship with the Lord. Reach out and grab grace by the hand today.

Pause to Reflect

- We all have sinned.
- God's grace is available through Jesus' sacrifice on the cross.
- Because of Jesus, we can receive forgiveness when we bring our sins to God.

Pause to Pray

Lord Jesus, I confess all of my sins to you. You took them on yourself on the cross, so I don't have to carry them. Please forgive me and cleanse me. Help me to honor you with my life. Thank you for grace. In Jesus' name I pray. Amen.

A Good God

"The mountains may depart and the hills be removed,
but my steadfast love shall not depart from you, and my
covenant of peace shall not be removed," says the LORD,
who has compassion on you.

ISAIAH 54:10 ESV

Miriam was the definition of determination. She carried herself with confidence and poise. But the more time we spent together, the more I had a growing momma instinct to tuck her under my wing. Miriam's facade of self-assurance hid a wounded soul.

At the bar of my kitchen, she explained that her kids' father abruptly left them. He was only one in a long line of men who crushed her heart. When other girls her age were concerned about Barbies and baby dolls, Miriam lived in nightly terror. The groping hands of her cousin stole pieces of her innocence for four years. Miriam was abandoned by her parents as a teen and raised by an affluent uncle. However, the new family treated Miriam and her two siblings as outsiders. Miriam saved enough money to set out on her own at nineteen. Determined to live a better life, she brought her siblings into a small apartment to raise them alone.

An incident after a night out with friends tore the last pieces of her heart. Though she didn't date much, Miriam reluctantly accepted a ride from an acquaintance following the event. The man gave her a sedation drug on the way home. Then he abused her, threw her from the car, and left her unconscious on the side of the road. She lay there until a stranger found her. In fact, that's the way she felt her whole life: abused, unwanted, and alone.

As I listened to the story, the reluctance in Miriam's relationship with God made sense. Few people had been loyal to her. Leaning over my coffee, I gently assured her that the Lord never abandons his children. He was faithful to heal the wounds if given access to her heart. For months I watched Miriam bravely pursue God despite the fears. Brokenness slowly molded into wholeness. Bitterness washed away to reveal joy. She experienced genuine love possibly for the first time.

Through my relationship with Miriam, I began to question why many of us push God away. I have also loved him at arms' length at times. While browsing blogs from my desk, I came across an article titled "When He Leaves."[17] The headline jolted my attention, but I wasn't sure why. I read it repeatedly. *When He Leaves. When He Leaves.* Then I realized… *he left.* Many of us have had our precious hearts broken when he, whoever that may be, left. And we felt alone holding shattered pieces of our soul in our laps. The absence of any close relationship can cause these intense feelings of isolation. If not mindful, we can filter life through the kaleidoscope of our pain.

What happens when the people who are supposed to be constant in life leave? Or they are present but emotionally detached? All of these factors can contribute to a *fear of abandonment,* which is possibly the most common and damaging fears of all.[18] Studies show that 57 percent of Americans are currently grieving the loss of a loved one within the last three years.[19] Based on the research, a large majority of us can be experiencing abandonment issues. This often leads to difficulty trusting and being intimate in relationships.[20]

I have allowed the failures of others to affect my view of God. However, my abandonment fears do not define my heavenly Father. Revelation 19:11 says that his name is *Faithful and True.* God promises more than seven times in Scripture to never abandon his children. That's a promise for each day of the week. Do not let struggles hide God's goodness from you, friend. He can be trusted to keep his word.

49

Miriam recently stood at the altar with a solid and reliable man. As they said, "I do," a familiar verse drifted across my mind: "He will not leave you nor forsake you" (Deuteronomy 31:8 NKJV). God is loyally by your side, fiercely working on your behalf, and eternally good. God never fails.

Pause to Reflect

- Absences of loved ones can cause abandonment-related fears, which often translate into our relationship with God.
- God is not a human who can falter, lie, or neglect.
- There is a promise of the faithfulness of God in Scripture for each day of the week.

Pause to Pray

Father, when I'm afraid that you will leave or fail, please remind me of your faithfulness and power. You are good when others are not. You never forget me. Thank you for your constant loving support. Help me to rely on you. In Jesus' name I pray. Amen.

The Purpose

"God is trying to call us back to that for which He created us—to worship Him and to enjoy Him forever!"[21]
A. W. TOZER

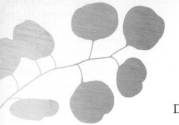

The One Thing

Whom have I in heaven but you?
I desire you more than anything on earth.
<small>PSALM 73:25 NLT</small>

I imagined that Martha frantically whirled around the house. The distant crowd shouted Jesus' name as the Lord entered her little village of Bethany. Jesus and his disciples would be arriving any minute at the home she shared with her siblings, Lazarus and Mary.

Martha wasn't inside while Jesus shared stories that filled the room with laughter and awe. She was out by the fire preparing dinner. Martha longed to hear about Jesus' miracles, too, but someone had to make the food. She looked to delegate some of the responsibilities. But wait. Where was Mary? Peering in the window, Martha gasped when her eyes landed on her sister. Was she audacious enough to sit at the feet of the rabbi? Why wasn't she helping? Martha mentally lectured Mary while slamming the dishes.

Martha was furious and wanted to burst through the door and make a scene. Not wanting Jesus to think poorly of her, she took a breath, smoothed her apron, and entered the room. "Master, is it fair that I'm doing all the cooking while Mary sits here? Please tell her to get up and do something to help me." Martha stopped before coarse words spilled out with her emotions.

Jesus understood that culture discouraged women from being disciples, but he did not chastise Mary. Instead, he turned to Martha and said, "My dear Martha, you are worried and upset over all these details! There is only one thing worth being concerned about. Mary has discovered it, and it will not be taken away from her" (Luke 10:41–42 NLT).

Can you imagine Jesus coming to your house? I would probably be Magic Eraser-ing the walls, baseboards, and whatever that sticky substance is on the table. Martha often gets a bad rap for wanting to work while her sister worships. Yet, Jesus' words put her perfectionism into perspective. The dinner, the dishes, or even the dilemma were not what was important. Mary had discovered the meaning of life at Jesus' feet. Like Martha, the details of the day may pull our focus from the purpose we were created for. It may feel like we exist for many things, but we were made for one thing: an intimate relationship with the Lord. All of the other parts of life flow from our connection with God.

Let's pause and rewind the script from our story of Martha to the few weeks before in the life of Jesus. Not long before Jesus visited the two sisters, he empowered the disciples to feed five thousand men with five loaves of bread and two fish. If we added women and children to the head count, the number possibly totaled over twenty thousand people (9:10–17). Then Jesus walked on water on the Sea of Galilee (Matthew 14:22–33). He also gave Peter the ability to walk on the waves. Following those events, Jesus took his closest disciples to the top of a mountain where they saw him supernaturally illuminated in glorious light. They watched in awe as he conversed with the Old Testament prophets, Elijah and Moses (Luke 9:28–35). Only a short time after that, Jesus arrived at Martha's house.

I wonder what would have happened if Martha decided that dinner could wait while she received from the Lord? If Jesus empowered the disciples to feed twenty thousand people with a bit of bread and fish, how many could he have fed through Martha's hands that day? If the Lord gave Peter the ability to walk on water, I wonder what miraculous abilities Martha might have experienced? If Jesus crossed time barriers to visit with prophets of old, how might he have multiplied Martha's time?

Let's be with the Lord today. Chaos flees when sitting at the feet of Jesus. Intimacy with God injects joy into the rest of our day. Peace is found in the power of his presence.

Pause to Reflect

- Our primary purpose is to have a relationship with God.
- Jesus has the power to stretch minutes, resources, and abilities.
- Time with God is always productive.

Pause to Pray

Lord Jesus, I desire to be near you. I dedicate myself to spending time in your presence. Please cover the rest of my day with grace and power as I walk with you. In Jesus' name I pray. Amen.

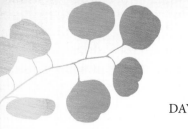

Grace in the Desert

I can never escape from your Spirit! I can never get away from your presence! If I go up to heaven, you are there; if I go down to the grave, you are there. If I ride the wings of the morning, if I dwell by the farthest oceans, even there your hand will guide me, and your strength will support me.

PSALM 139:7–10 NLT

Emma was a terrible sleeper. She would wake us up nearly every night of the week. As a toddler, she would stumble to my bedside around two a.m. and whisper with a lisp, "Mommy, can you pray for me?" That's cute the first fifteen or twenty times. Sleepily, I suggested that she needed to learn to pray for herself. Don't judge. She continued to night-wander until she was almost four.

Our next baby, Evan, suffered worse sleep anxiety than Emma. He would tap my shoulder in the middle of the night and whisper-yell, "Mom, I can't sleep." For five years, BJ and I felt like we rarely had peaceful rest. During that time, my prayers reflected the desperation of sleep deprivation. As I chugged coffee and held up heavy eyes, I talked and cried with the Lord. He listened and revealed creative ways to connect with him throughout the day. Overwhelming seasons can make spiritual growth seem impossible.

Stress is a growing epidemic. Nearly half of women say that they endure fatigue, have headaches, and feel like crying due to stress.[22] Prolonged periods of pressure and anxiety can seem like being lost in a desert. Life can feel dry, bitter, and barren as we desperately search for an oasis. God did not design his children to be desert dwellers. We were made to pass through dry places.

The Israelites found themselves wandering through a dry wasteland. After their freedom from slavery in Egypt, the Israelites should have passed through the Sinai Desert on the way to the promised land. An intended two-week trip ended up a forty-year journey in a region that can exceed 100 degrees. Although they went the long way around, God's grace didn't depart from his people. Scripture says he led them with a pillar of a cloud during the day and with a pillar of fire at night. People typically picture tall, cylindrical shapes of a cloud and fire. However, *pillar* in Hebrew can also mean "a platform" or "flat structure." I believe that the cloud drifted over the Israelites during the day, shading them from the scorching sun. The fire hovered over them at night, warming the desert chill. God also provided for their needs with food that miraculously fell from the sky called *manna*. He satisfied their thirst with water that flowed from a rock. Scripture says that their shoes never wore out. Like a faithful father to his children, the Lord led his people by the hand. God gives grace to survive and thrive in the desert.

Today, you may feel like you're sinking in sand dunes. It's easy to feel distant from God during seasons of drought. Prioritizing purpose can seem impossible when living in survival mode. However, I want you to remember that God's grace is sufficient in dry seasons. He will protect you from the scorching sun of frustration and the chill of hopelessness. Growing closer to God through the desert will be possible as you follow him. I encourage you to prioritize prayer as you pass through the land of difficulty. Grace will multiply your time and effort. God's presence can give you strength that you didn't know was possible. Spiritual nourishment can fall and flow from unexpected sources. The Lord loves to communicate with his children in innovative ways. Cling to him as he leads you out of places that feel barren and into abundance. God's covering grace empowers you to grow.

Pause to Reflect

- Seasons of stress and anxiety can feel scorching to the soul.
- Growing our relationship with God can feel difficult in stressful situations.
- Grace empowers us for spiritual growth during tough times as we draw close to God.

Pause to Pray

Lord, during hard days, I ask for grace. My heart is to be close to you in every season. Please stretch my time and efforts as I follow you. Revive me in your presence. In Jesus' name I pray. Amen.

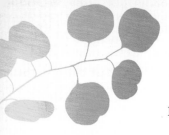

A Life of Purpose

*Yes, feast on all the treasures of the heavenly realm and
fill your thoughts with heavenly realities, and not with
the distractions of the natural realm.*

COLOSSIANS 3:2 TPT

Sara's presence lit up a room. Her pain seemed to
magnify her magnetic personality. The first moment
we met is imprinted on my heart.

Conversation filled the living room as ladies of
all ages met for our fall Bible study group. The phone
rang as I was finishing up my brunch dish. Jennifer,
a regular attendee, called to let me know that Sara
would be joining us that day. And that Sara had stage
four breast cancer.

Stage four…those words carried a weightiness
that contrasted the joy in the room. I gathered my
faith and tried to steady my emotions. As the door
swung open, I was taken aback by Sara's brilliant
smile. Chemo had taken her hair but clearly not her

hope. Throwing her arms around me she welcomed herself inside like we were old friends.

Sara's sassy yet sensitive nature touched our group. Occasionally she would miss Bible study, not because she didn't want to be there, but chemo sessions pulled her away. Declarations of faith filled her stories and even her tears as she shared her heart. I can't count the times that her contagious joy interrupted our conversations. The overflow of her time with the Lord and his gentle encouragement poured through her words.

Fall came to a close and made way for a new Bible study semester. Sara arrived again, but this time she was thinner and her face drawn in. Short curls of hair covered her head as doctors had stopped the unsuccessful chemo treatments. Her body was visibly tired, but her faith was resolute. Sara's extended stay in the hospital kept her from finishing the semester.

Sara's condition quickly declined. In a matter of weeks, I received the call that she was moving to hospice care. Next to her bedside, I held her swollen hand as we sang worship songs and prayed. Her love for God flooded into her last moments. Three days later, Sara went to heaven still holding tightly to Jesus.

I don't understand why my friend passed away, but I know that Sara remained full of hope despite her failing health. Illness and suffering brought her life into focus. She knew her purpose and knew it well.

Like Sara, what if we lived like life is temporary? How would our days and weeks be designed differently? Our calendars are often crammed full of things that feel important but have little impact. The result is a life built on busyness instead of purpose.

Far too often, to-do lists and unnecessary details hijack my attention. My mind races as I rush from place to place. In this state, my vision locks on the next project to tackle. Can you relate? Do you ever feel like you're just here to change diapers, clean floors, or fill orders? What would it look like to live fully present in your purpose?

Mindlessly humming through emails one day, I cleared one message after another. Delete. Delete. Del—wait. The subject snagged my attention: "What's the Meaning of Life in America?" The research revealed that 69 percent of Americans find their significance in family, 34 percent in their careers, and another 23 percent in money.[23] Turning to our families, jobs, and finances as the meaning of life seems natural because they are what demand our attention every day. Although these are important, our heart calls for more. Planted deep within is a longing for our time to be filled with more depth than demands.

Purpose begins with pursuing an intimate relationship with God. The rest of our decisions and details flow out of a place of intimacy with him. Sara knew that life makes more sense when lived in God's love. Let's resist the distractions and devote our days to the one who is worthy of adoration. Purpose is found in God's presence.

Pause to Reflect

- Humans were designed with a core need for God.
- Problems and projects often try to distract us from our purpose.
- The primary meaning of life is to live in a relationship with the Lord.

Pause to Pray

Lord Holy Spirit, sometimes details pull my attention away from what matters most. Please help me prioritize my relationship with you. My main purpose in life is to know you intimately, and my greatest fulfillment is found in your presence. In Jesus' name I pray. Amen.

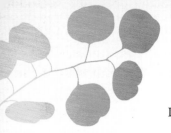

Friends with Purpose

*Enjoy the companionship of those
who call on the Lord with pure hearts.*
2 TIMOTHY 2:22 NLT

Playing hide-and-seek from my torrential to-do list, I flipped on the TV to an old episode of *Friends*. Rachel, Ross, Phoebe, and Chandler sat in the living room on Thanksgiving Day while Monica lectured the group. At the grand height of her speech, Joey burst open the door and entered wearing a pair of ridiculous plaid pants. "Joey, those are my maternity pants," yelled Phoebe.

"No, no. These are my Thanksgiving pants," Joey said, wide-eyed as he stretched out the elastic belly and headed to conquer the turkey.[24] I nearly choked on my tea.

There's a reason why you can watch *Friends* almost any time of the day. During its ten-year span, the sitcom won more than sixty awards, including six Emmys.[25] For a decade, we listened to the friends argue on that orange couch in Central Perk. More than fifty-two million Americans tuned in to the show's final goodbye, making it the fifth most-watched series finale of all time.[26] At the end of an era, viewers were left with the question: What made this show so wildly popular?

One answer may have to do with the depth of the friends' relationships with each other. They were so close that, in 238 episodes, the friends rarely knocked on Monica's purple door when entering the apartment. At any given moment, they would fling the door open and head to the fridge. Only the best of friends have that kind of liberty. I can identify who's at my door by how many times their toddler rings the bell. However, I think the writers of the show were on to something when they intentionally kept the friends from knocking. Aren't those the close-knit, carefree relationships we desire? I'm not encouraging you to burst into someone's apartment without warning, but we long for friends who have an open invitation into our world. Rare gems in life are people who answer our call and know how we're doing by the tone of the *hey*. We are attracted to where we are authentically known. Unfortunately, many of us feel that those significant relationships are absent.

In America, loneliness plagues people of all ages. A Harvard study shows that 61 percent of young adults and 51 percent of moms with small children report feeling serious loneliness.[27] Quality friendships are not always easy to make and maintain. Nearly half of people report that shyness makes it difficult to make friends.[28] Another third of the population say that their commitments to family poses a problem to building relationships.[29] An additional 28 percent say that a lack of hobbies makes friend-time difficult.[30] While we all may experience these challenges, forming lasting friendships is worth the effort.

Quality relationships enrich our lives with beautiful benefits. Friends are support systems when all falls apart. Hangout time releases happy hormones like endorphins and oxytocin.[31] Scripture promises emotional healing and encouragement when we pray for one another (James 5:16). We are often the happiest and healthiest when supported by meaningful friendships.

For many of us, the question is not *how to be a good friend* but *how to find time to be one*. Accidentally stumbling upon time for friends is not likely. Intentionality and sometimes creativity are needed to develop quality relationships. My friends and I, with our busy schedules, have actually gone to the grocery store together to connect. We have sat on living room couches with kids crawling over us. Weekend getaways that were way too hard to plan are now sweet memories. Valuing time together, extending grace, and being flexible helps to build lasting friendships.

God did not design you to live in isolation. Remember that the Holy Spirit is always close when loneliness looms like a shadow. He is the primary supplier of all needs, including friends. Your heavenly Father will provide people who support your purpose if you ask him. Godly friends pray, build up, and speak life. They are supports that reinforce your calling. Don't do life alone. Today, consider reaching out to an old friend and, perhaps, making a new one.

Pause to Reflect

- Quality friendships have both natural and spiritual benefits.
- Godly friends may not be perfect, but they support your relationship with the Lord.
- God provides for our needs, which includes friends.

Pause to Pray

Lord, when I feel lonely, your sweet presence is always nearby. Please surround me with a support system of people who encourage me spiritually. Thank you for the friends I already have and for the ones that you are sending. In Jesus' name I pray. Amen.

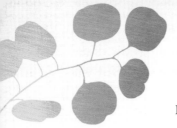

The Gift

"Thus says the LORD...Call to me and I will answer you, and will tell you great and hidden things that you have not known."

JEREMIAH 33:2–3 ESV

Being in a foreign country without my family made my birthday feel strange. I stared out the bus window as we crisscrossed our way through Bethlehem. It didn't feel coincidental that I was in Jesus' place of birth on my birthday.

Weeks before my trip to Israel, I prayed about a gift I wanted to purchase. No one but God knew about this request. I asked for a ring inscribed with, *You have come to the kingdom for such a time as this*, in Hebrew. The verse from the book of Esther was close to my heart. The ring I pictured was a silver spiral band, and I held hope that God would get it for me.

Back on the bus in Bethlehem, I looked down at my empty right hand. I wasn't sure where to purchase the ring or, if given the opportunity, how much it would cost. A ding from my phone interrupted my thoughts. A friend texted to say that she was sending me birthday money. I thanked her and said that I knew just what to buy.

Two days later, the tour ventured into Jerusalem for shopping. My main mission was to find my ring. The tour guide wandered by, and I asked him if there were shops that inscribed custom jewelry. He replied, "There's only one. I'll take you there." Inside the boutique, I scanned the shelves. A silver spiral ring caught my attention. I nervously approached the counter unsure of how to communicate my request. The salesperson happened to be a Jewish-American girl. She pulled out a Bible from below the counter that had Hebrew and English text side-by-side. Skimming down the pages, she found the Hebrew version of my verse. After she placed the order, I gasped when I glanced at the bill. The total was the same amount as my friend's birthday money. Weeks later my ring arrived. My heart warmed as I slid it on my finger. God had this gift planned for me before I asked him.

The desires of our heart matter to the Lord. Although they may not be set in sterling silver, God gives us custom-crafted gifts each time we pray. He meets us in prayer with priceless presents of peace, encouragement, and strength. Each gift fits perfectly to our needs and is wrapped in his love.

Prayer is an invitation to encounter the living God. It is more intimate than a list of routine recitations. Prayer is a two-way conversation with the one who spoke creation into existence. God is never boring and loves to listen. The Lord knows your needs before you ask (Matthew 6:8) and delights in every detail of your life (Psalm 37:23).

Not knowing what to say can be a roadblock to prayer. One of Jesus' disciples had this same concern when he asked, "Lord, teach us to pray" (Luke 11:1 NIV). Jesus answered with what we call the Lord's Prayer. Each phrase gently instructs us how to connect with the Father. When I read Matthew 6:9–13 (NKJV), I pictured Jesus lifting his eyes in worship as he said, "Our Father in heaven, Hallowed be Your name." His heart hungered for God's perfect plans when he declared, "Your kingdom come. Your will be done On earth as it is in heaven." The group's needs mattered as he asked, "Give us this day our daily bread." Although he was sinless, Jesus expressed the disciples' need for forgiveness of sin and to release the wrongs of others. "And forgive us our debts, As we forgive our debtors." The group probably nodded in agreement as he asked for protection, "And do not lead us into temptation, But deliver us from the evil one." Jesus may have raised his hands as he closed with praise, "For Yours is the kingdom and the power and the glory forever." The gathering undoubtedly agreed with a hearty,

"Amen!" or *So be it*. Jesus led by example in living a life of prayer.

God has treasures tucked away within your time with him. All he asks for in return is your heart.

Pause to Reflect

- God cares about our needs and desires.
- The Holy Spirit brings tailor-made gifts to our prayer time.
- The Lord's Prayer is more of a roadmap than a recitation.

Pause to Pray

Father, I want to experience the gifts you have for me in prayer. Help me receive from your presence. I know you listen each time I call to you. In Jesus' name I pray. Amen.

The Heart

*"I never have any difficulty believing in miracles,
since I experienced the miracle of a change
in my own heart."*

<small>AUGUSTINE</small>

The Father's Heart

Look with wonder at the depth of the Father's marvelous love that he has lavished on us! He has called us and made us his very own beloved children.

1 JOHN 3:1 TPT

Jim was a self-made millionaire. He could be found in his top-floor office by sunrise. The toe of his snakeskin boots turned up a bit from kneeling in prayer as light filtered over the Houston skyline.

Jim loved working with his two daughters. Jaqueline led the accounting department. He adored her steadiness and attention to detail, but she lacked the fire in her eyes like Evangeline. Jim grinned each time his youngest daughter pinned back her red locks and played boardroom hardball with incoming executives. Yet he could still see the freckled little girl who brought him tiny teacups on saucers. He was just as proud of her then as he was in those boardroom battles.

One morning, Jim entered his office in the dark and found Evangeline sitting at his desk. She leaned back in his chair. "Morning, Daddy. Can we talk?" Jim clicked the door behind him. "I want to discuss my shares of the company stock. I want to cash out now." Evangeline looked her father square in the eyes.

Caught off guard, Jim asked, "Honey, what's wrong? Do you need money? I thought you would one day take over and—"

"Jacqueline can have the business. I've made my decision." Jim sat speechless as Evangeline pushed past him. He called his attorney, signed the paperwork, and gave Evangeline what she had asked for.

Jim called Evangeline the next day, but it went straight to voicemail. He texted but no response. Evangeline's social media accounts were all blocked. Rumors from friends placed Evangeline on a yacht with a football star. Tabloids showed her in A-list nightclubs with revolving men by her side. Each morning Jim kneeled and prayed for his daughter.

Nine months passed with no word from Evangeline. One evening Jim was signing off on an email when his phone rang from an unknown number. "Daddy?" Evangeline's voice cracked on the other end.

"Oh, honey! Are you okay? Where are you?"

Her words came back slowly. "I'm okay, Daddy. I'm downstairs. Can…Can I come home?"

Jim bolted from his office. In the company lobby stood Evangeline with her phone in hand, her red curls trimmed short to her head, freckled cheeks tear streaked, and a perfectly rounded belly. Jim didn't see the stares of the staff or hear their whispers. He rushed to his daughter, and Evangeline sobbed into her father's chest.

"I'm so sorry, Daddy. I thought things would be better—"

"Shhh. I'm glad you're okay. Welcome home, sweetheart."

What a portrait of God's heart toward you and me. While Jim and his daughters are fictional, they are based on Jesus' famous parable, the prodigal son. Found in Luke 15, the story captures the images of a son's rebellion and his father's forgiveness. Like Evangeline, the young man demanded an inheritance early and wasted it on wild living. When the money ran out, he found himself living in filth. Certain that being a servant in his father's house was better than the streets, the young man returned home. Scripture says that while the son was still far away, the father's eyes were scanning the hills. When he caught a glimpse of the son's shadow, the father took off running at full speed. He restored the young man with the finest robe, sandals for his feet, and a signet ring with the family crest. When the world would have shunned his rebellion as disgraceful, the father celebrated the return of his son.

Lift your head when shame tries to cast a shadow over your soul. If you feel unwelcome in your Father's house, I encourage you to turn to the Lord. He embraces all who call on him. God grants access to the promises in Scripture to his children. Like the dad in the parable, the eyes of the Lord scan the hilltops in search of a soul who needs him. The Father runs to a surrendered heart every time.

Pause to Reflect

- When we want to hide in humility, God wants us to receive grace.
- The Father exchanges labels of shame and dishonor with titles of *son* and *daughter*.
- The best the world has to offer cannot compare to the blessings found in the Father's house.

Pause to Pray

Heavenly Father, when I feel unworthy, I choose to turn to you. You never resist a surrendered heart. I ask you to forgive all my failures and poor choices. I receive your grace and take my place as your child. In Jesus' name I pray. Amen.

A Healthy Heart

He restores my soul.
PSALM 23:3 ESV

Doctors and nurses rushed around Brian's three-pound body. He was not supposed to be born for five more weeks. The staff had detected an abnormal heart murmur. Brian was diagnosed with an atrial septal defect, also known as a hole in the heart. A doctor explained, "We'll need to fix his heart when he's a little older, maybe six months." The diagnosis seemed far too simple for such a sick boy.

Brian's mom did not hold her son for the first few days of his life. More than one month was needed for his fragile body to stabilize. On the day of his release, Mom fumbled with swaddling the tiny infant in the blanket. "He's just so—the blanket is so big. I don't know if we're ready."

Brian's mom allowed the nurse to step in. "He's going to be okay, Mom."

Brian kept getting worse. At six weeks old, he struggled to breathe and turned a pale shade of blue. The pediatrician ordered that Brian see a specialist. "Essentially, your son has a congenital heart defect in addition to the hole in his heart. His aortic artery connects to the wrong side." The doctor listed a host of problems. "This needs to be fixed right away."

Brian underwent major surgery to restore his heart to a healthy condition at seven weeks old and six pounds. Mom froze at the recovery room door as monitors filled the room. Tubes and tape engulfed her son. The calming voice of the surgeon helped her relax for the first time in months. "Don't worry, Mom. He's breathing all on his own. He's going to be just fine."

Brian strengthened after heart surgery. As a teenager he played baseball with his friends most days after school. He went on to graduate college, marry, and have children. His mom said, "The Lord gave Brian a new heart."

The heart is the epicenter of human life. Two definitions are common for the word *heart*. There is the obvious physical heart that is responsible for bringing life throughout our body. There is also a non-physical, invisible heart that explains the source of our feelings and desires. It makes sense that the two are named identically as they have similar functions. In the same way that blood is filtered and sent out by our heart organ, the contents of our invisible heart affect our entire life. In Proverbs, King Solomon used this illustration to issue a wise warning: "Above all else, guard your heart, for everything you do flows from it" (Proverbs 4:23 NIV). A person's mind, will, and emotions make up their invisible heart. These three things together are what we also call *the soul*.

The soul is often confused with a person's spirit, but they are not the same. The apostle Paul separated the spirit and soul by saying, "May your whole spirit and soul and body be kept blameless until our Lord Jesus Christ comes again" (1 Thessalonians 5:23 NLT). Our spirit connects us to God. It is the highway by which we receive peace, forgiveness, and rest. While these things are received from God through the human spirit, they are filtered through and sent into our life by the soul.

Although most of us will not experience Brian's medical condition, we all can have gaping holes in our hearts. If left unhealed, these hurts can affect us in adulthood. Child abuse, divorce, and injustices can critically wound our delicate souls. Sometimes injuries like betrayal, adultery, or financial ruin create wounds. Some holes are small enough to go unnoticed, but significant injuries require the healing of the heavenly surgeon.

A hurting soul can cause resistance in our relationship with God. Wounds within can weaken our ability to receive encouragement from the Holy Spirit.

Let's ask the Lord to reveal any holes in our hearts. Be brave and bring the pain to God. A healthy life begins with a heart that is being made whole.

Pause to Reflect

- We need the Lord to identify and heal any heart conditions.
- The contents of our soul spreads to our entire being.
- Holes in the invisible heart can make it challenging to grow in our relationship with God.

Pause to Pray

Lord, it's important that my heart is spiritually healthy. I don't want harmful things to spread from my soul. Instead, I want your Spirit to bring life to my entire being. Please heal all my hurts and give me a healthy heart. In Jesus' name I pray. Amen.

Heart Transplant

The LORD is close to the brokenhearted;
he rescues those whose spirits are crushed.
The righteous person faces many troubles,
but the LORD comes to the rescue each time.

PSALM 34:18–19 NLT

John grips his hostage by the neck, raises his gun, and commands the police to lay down their weapons. "I am not going to bury my son. My son will bury me." The crowd responds in an approving roar as helicopters circle overhead. John drags the hostage, a battered SWAT officer, backward toward the hospital door.

The veteran police officer yells back, "This is not going to end well for you, John. There's only two ways out of here: jail and dead. What's it going to be?"

In the movie *John Q.*, life had backed John Archibald into an angry corner after his son, Mike, collapsed on the baseball field. He and his wife, Denise, learned that Mike would die without a

$200,000 heart transplant surgery. If the initial blow of Mike's diagnosis wasn't enough, the hospital staff explained that the Archibald's insurance did not cover the treatment.

John was informed that he and Denise must raise $75,000 for the procedure. When they were unable to produce the amount, the hospital released Mike who was near death. Gun in hand, John rushed into the emergency room in a desperate move to find a heart for his son. He smashed the security cameras and padlocked the door. John's last hope clung to exchanging the hospital staff and patients for Mike's new heart.

Now inside the ER, only a short time passes before the phone rings. John refuses to mediate terms with the hostage negotiator. "I want my kid's name on the donors' list. You got that?" He slams the phone to the counter. The standoff begins as John fights to find a donor match for Mike, and time is short.

As night falls, John shares an emotional phone call with his son. Mike whispers, "Dad, am I going to die?" John realizes his only option is to give his own heart to Mike. He reaches into his pocket for a bullet and loads the gun.

A hostage speaks up, "Wait a minute. Are you telling me that gun was empty the whole time?"

John says, "Yeah, I'm all talk. The only one I ever considered killing was me." The surgeon stands by as John lays on the gurney.

John jerks the gun to his head and pulls the trigger. Silence. He clutches his chest and unclicks the safety. John raises the gun again and places his finger on the trigger.

"John!" Denise screams through tears. "It's a miracle! They found a heart!" She holds the donor list to the ER window. In a moving scene, John is permitted to watch Mike receive his new heart before being taken into police custody.

Months later outside a courtroom, a healthy Mike flexes his muscles to his dad. As John rides away in a squad car, Mike rounds his arms like a wrestler and mouths, "Thank you."[32]

Throughout the film, John displayed extraordinary love for his son. Without a heart transplant, Mike would have died, but that outcome was unacceptable to his dad. John risked everything, including his own heart, to replace Mike's broken one.

The heavenly Father grieves when his children's hearts are broken. Scripture assures us that God is close when we're hurting. Every tear matters to him (Psalm 56:8). The Lord wraps our wounds in his love. God will go to great lengths to see us whole again.

Jesus paid the price for your heart transplant on the cross. His broken heart was payment for your healed one. If you're hurting today, I encourage you to tell God how you feel. Pour out the pain to him in prayer. He cares about all of it (Psalm 37:23). Once the hurt is emptied, consider waiting for his response. Allow his nearness to wash over your wounds. God exchanges broken hearts with his own.

Pause to Reflect

- Jesus is acquainted with our sorrows, so he understands our pain.
- Jesus' death on the cross paid the price for our total healing.
- God replaces the pain of a broken heart with his peace.

Pause to Pray

Heavenly Father, when my heart is hurting, I turn to you. I give you all the sorrow and grief. I open myself to you, the master surgeon. By Christ's death on the cross, I receive peace today. Whether healing comes at once or one day at a time, I will be healed. In Jesus' name I pray. Amen.

Remove the Rocks

I will walk with you in complete freedom,
for I seek to follow your every command.
PSALM 119:45 TPT

Thoughts of rejection and questioning my worth
had been surfacing in my mind. Tired of feeling
unwanted and broken, I landed on the blue sofa in
my pastor's office. He leaned in and listened to my
story. When my words ran dry, he responded, "I think
there are stones in your heart that need to come out.
Like a pebble in the shoe, they're unnoticeable until
they move. If you step on them, it hurts and causes a
reaction."

"Stones? I...I don't understand. I don't feel any
hardness or anger toward people who have hurt me,"
I said.

"You can forgive someone, which is important.
But forgiving doesn't always heal the injuries they left
behind, which can harden pieces of your heart," he

explained. Although I didn't fully grasp his response, I agreed to follow along.

Pastor guided me through a prayer acknowledging the wounds wrenching my heart. As we pushed forward, I felt the Holy Spirit reveal some of the trauma buried in my soul. Images of past hurts came to mind and their connections to my current struggles. Pain I never knew existed poured out in hot tears. In the end it seemed like Jesus had reached in, pulled out rocks, and tossed them away. God's acceptance washed over me. Wholeness warmed through my heart.

Many people have recurring emotions like rejection and unworthiness. These feelings are often triggered by reactions to hidden hurts. Triggers typically result from past traumatic events[33] that produce intense emotional responses.[34] Common reactions may be feelings of abandonment, betrayal, or insecurity.[35] These emotions can rob our peace and jerk away our joy. They also have an impact on our relationship with God. Stones in the soul can block truth from taking root and producing evidence of God's love in our lives.

The patio and the breeze made a perfect setting as I slid open my Bible one morning and turned to Mark 4:1–9. As I read, I pictured the waves of the Galilean Sea lapping on the beach. Jesus stood in a boat and spoke to the crowd on the hillside. "Listen! A farmer went out to plant some seed." The audience nodded regarding the familiarity of his story. "Some of the seed fell on a footpath and the birds came and ate it." They squinted at the gulls swarming overhead. "Other seed fell on the shallow soil with underlying rock." Some of the crowd lifted their feet to reveal black stones below. "The seed sprouted quickly…but the plant soon wilted under the hot sun and since it didn't have deep roots, it died."

The farmers groaned. "You have to remove the rocks first," one of them shouted.

Jesus continued, "Other seed fell among thorns that choked out the plants so they produced no grain." The group inched away from the six-foot thistle weeds on the hillside. "Still other seed fell on fertile soil… and produced a crop that was thirty, sixty, and even a hundred times as much as had been planted." Families smiled at the thought of an abundant harvest season. Then Jesus closed his story with an authoritative statement: "Anyone with ears to hear should listen and understand."[36]

As Jesus taught what we now call the parable of the sower, the types of soils in his story represented four conditions of the heart. The seed symbolized the Word of God. He explained these heart conditions to his disciples privately.

Although Jesus unpacked each soil type, it was the second that moved me the most. God's Word seeps down into our soul, but embedded stones restrict truth from growing deep roots. These rocks are often harmful thoughts that stemmed from past pain. You're not good enough. People will hurt you. Why doesn't anyone want me? These thoughts can all be stones in the heart. Jesus wants the life-giving Word to develop a harvest of hope in us.

Let us surrender the condition of our soul to God. Ask him to reveal any hurts and hindrances that reside beneath the surface. Sometimes a conversation with a pastor, friend, or counselor may lead us to healing. Love, joy, and peace will bloom as Scripture sinks deep and develops roots.

Pause to Reflect

- Painful past experiences can create wounds in the soul.
- Hurts can become like rocks in our hearts that cause sharp reactions when touched by conversations or events.
- God wants us to live healed, healthy, and hopeful.

Pause to Pray

Lord, please reveal any rocks in the soil of my heart. Gently remove all hurt beneath the surface. Replace the wounds with your truth. Produce the fruit of a godly life within me. In Jesus' name I pray. Amen.

DAY 20

Forgive

*Watch over each other to make sure that no one misses
the revelation of God's grace. And make sure no one lives
with a root of bitterness sprouting within them which
will only cause trouble and poison the hearts of many.*
HEBREWS 12:15 TPT

Unforgiveness held Anna captive. It was under-
standable why she clung so tightly to the key. Not
many could let go of a story like hers.

"Now Anna, you're marryin' this young man.
You know how important it is to join a good family,"
her father said.

"Yes, sir," eighteen-year-old Anna respectfully
responded, despite her hidden anguish. She didn't
want to be married, but family farm connections were
important in the Jackson Prairie plains of Mississippi
in the 1930s. The wedding was performed a week later
by the Baptist preacher in town. Anna was sent to a

one-bedroom house on her in-law's land with her new husband, Marshall.

Marshall was outgoing in public but a monster behind closed doors. Anna was expected to be a good wife, working to help with the family bills, cooking, cleaning, maintaining the laundry, and having sex with Marshall when he pleased. Marshall wasn't fond of moonshine or cigars but found solace in hitting Anna. Even after their children were born, the beatings, rage, and rape continued. Anna thought if she put their youngest daughter, Cora, in the bed with them, he would leave her alone. He didn't.

One morning after a brutal night, Anna waited until Marshall left for work, then she dialed the police station with trembling hands. "Sir, please help me. My husband is hittin' on me and I…I don't know what to do," she breathed heavily.

"Now, ma'am. He's the head of the house, and we don't like to meddle in family affairs," the officer said, dismissing her plea. None of her family or friends wanted to get involved either. For thirty years, Anna endured Marshall's brutality. Until one day, she snapped. Anna packed up their six children and left.

Decades later, Anna sat up in her nursing home bed to visit with her daughter. Cora couldn't help but notice that something was different. She had rarely seen her mother smile or laugh. Anna seemed lighter…

happy even. In a break in the conversation Anna leaned forward with a child-like grin. She said, "Well, I did it."

"Did what, Momma?" Cora asked.

"I forgave your daddy," Anna said as she patted her daughter's hand. One year later Anna went to be with Jesus. It was the happiest of her eighty-seven years of life.

Often unforgiveness imprisons the victim instead of the offender. In an attempt to punish the abuser, we often hang on to bitterness and harm ourselves instead. Harboring unforgiveness is like wrapping fingers around a hot curling iron but refusing to let go. Jesus said, "If you forgive those who sin against you, your heavenly Father will forgive you. But if you refuse to forgive others, your Father will not forgive your sins" (Matthew 6:14–15 NLT). Extending forgiveness to the person who hurt you doesn't absolve their actions. Only God does that. But it sets you free. Choosing to let go of pain and bitterness empties your heart to make room for God to pour in. Let it go. Let them go.

You may be thinking, *I just don't know how.* I get it. I, too, have wrestled with forgiving wrongs I never should have received. Jesus did too. Judas, a close disciple, sold the Savior and sent him to the cross. Before Jesus gave up his Spirit in death, he cried out, "Father, forgive them." He knows exactly how to release wrongdoings and will show you. A decision to let go and a private prayer to God begins the process: *Lord, I choose to forgive* _____.

Bitterness over yesterday steals our joy today. It robs us of the richness God wants to develop in our lives. Let's not wait until we are eighty-seven to let go of the hurt. Forgiveness is worth the fight.

Pause to Reflect

- The pain of the past steals our peace in the present.
- Jesus said that forgiveness for our sin hinges on our willingness to forgive others.
- Forgiveness is a process that starts with a choice to let go.

Pause to Pray

Lord Jesus, you know how it feels to be wounded by loved ones. And you understand my heartache too. It's not my responsibility to punish those who hurt me. When I refuse to forgive, I'm actually hurting myself. Lord, I choose to forgive _____. *Please help me. In Jesus' name I pray. Amen.*

The Spirit

"The human spirit fails,
except when the Holy Spirit fills."[37]
CORRIE TEN BOOM

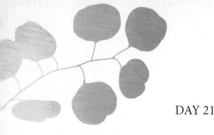

The Intersection

For his Spirit joins with our spirit
to affirm that we are God's children.
ROMANS 8:16 NLT

I bit my lip as I drummed my fingers on the car door
handle. We were searching for the highway, but the
road shrank with each turn. Our excursion in the
Colorado Rocky Mountains was not going as planned.
Phone signals dropped midway up the mountain, and
GPS refused to connect. The kids were going wild in
the backseat. I finally decided to state the obvious.
"Um, babe…I don't think this is the right way." We
argued about asking for directions. A few homes were
scattered across the mountainside, but the farther
we drove, the more intimidated we became. "These
look like those off-the-grid, doomsday people we see
on TV. The ones who are ready for the zombie apoc-
alypse. I don't think we should bang on their doors
uninvited," I said. We let the idea fall away.

A few more turns and the road stopped at muddy four-wheeler tracks that led into the forest. BJ put the car in reverse, the tires spun, and my heart skipped a beat. I imagined a bear or zombie-hunter would knock on the window any minute. BJ rocked the car forward. Then back. And forward again. Finally the wheels grabbed gravel, and we backed down the road. The skinny path left nowhere to turn around, so we inched the SUV in tight angles to change directions. One wrong move and we would have been back in the sludge or sliding down the mountain.

As the road widened, we relaxed. Finally, our tires touched pavement. Our cell phones regained service. Not much farther along, the trees opened, and we were able to see the interstate. I sat back, closed my eyes, and thought of how easily I took for granted something as simple as a highway until I got lost and needed one.

Roadways are connection points from one place to another. My best friend, Amazon Prime, is probably headed to my house on one right now. Similarly, there is a road that connects us with the Lord. We call it our *spirit*. This connection allows exchanges between the Holy Spirit and us. Fresh ideas, wisdom, and encouragement travel on it from God to those who seek his help. Like a path between two cities, our spirit joins us together with the Lord.

When desiring growth in a relationship with God, it is easy to get off course. Just like our trip into the mountains, we can get misdirected in spiritual growth. I have friends who try to access the Lord through mental thoughts and others who attempt to be closer to him by their works. I have done both in my life, but they didn't get me very far. Jesus explained it this way, "For God is Spirit, so those who worship him must worship in spirit and in truth" (John 4:24 NLT). Understanding this connection allows access to a deeper relationship with God. Misunderstanding it can send us down roads that aren't emotionally healthy or spiritually productive.

We often think of the spirit as something wild and magical. To say that a person *has spirit* usually means that they are passionate and strong-willed. Although we may desire to share their fiery passion, a person's spirit is different from these character-istics. Scripture says that we can control our spirit and learn how to direct it (1 Corinthians 14:32). Understanding truth comes from God by way of our human spirit (2:13). Through our connection with the Holy Spirit we can know the Lord's thoughts and become one with him (2:11; 6:17). All of these remarkable things and more are accessible through a relationship with God.

Friend, you don't have to strain to seek the Lord. He is near today and longs to spend time with you. Try quieting your thoughts and calming your emotions. Be still and give God room in your soul. A simple prayer will connect you to the Father. *Lord, would you draw me close today?* Life flows from the Spirit of God.

Pause to Reflect

- God is not mystical and difficult to know.
- The human spirit is what connects us to the Holy Spirit.
- Intimacy with God increases as we invest in spiritual growth.

Pause to Pray

Lord, I want to be near to you. Help me to come to you in spirit and in truth. Teach me how to grow my spirit so that I have a deeper connection with you. Help me to understand your ways so I can know you more intimately. In Jesus' name I pray. Amen.

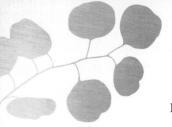

Living Water

They will neither hunger nor thirst. The searing sun will not reach them anymore. For the LORD in his mercy will lead them; he will lead them beside cool waters.

ISAIAH 49:10 NLT

I imagined that the woman peered through the stone-cut window from the shadows. Seeing the trail of women making their way to the well outside the city gates, she shrank back into the darkness. *It's still too early to go*, she thought, although her water supply ran out hours ago. Her husband muttered a shallow goodbye as he headed out for the day's work. Actually, he wasn't her husband at all, but after five failed marriages, she just couldn't bring herself to commit. Never again.

Parched lips urged her toward the well, and she hoisted her jug onto her head. The noonday sun stunned her eyes and pounded her shoulders as she left the safety of the shadows. Few in town noticed her. She preferred anonymity anyway.

In the haze of the sunshine, the woman made out what looked to be a man sitting on the edge of the well. Should she wait another hour? The man's blue and white shawl suggested he was a Jew, a rare sight in Shechem. She reasoned, *A Jewish rabbi would not acknowledge a Samaritan woman like me anyway*. The woman approached the well, head down. Shockingly, the man did speak to her. "Please give me a drink," he requested. *Why is he talking to me?* Instinct told her to run back to the darkness, but she was tired of running. Running from men. Running from shame.

Against her better judgment, she decided to respond. "Why are you asking me for a drink?" she snapped back.

The sarcasm seemed to go unnoticed as Jesus rose and replied, "If you knew the gift God has for you and who you are speaking to, you would ask me, and I would give you living water." A chilling breeze brushed between them.

These cryptic words called to her, but the woman wasn't sure why. She thought, *A spring of water in this arid land? Could this be true? I would never be thirsty and would never have to return to this well. Their judging glances and demeaning whispers would disappear.* The woman wasn't sure what plan was next, but she was all in.[38]

This woman's conversation with Jesus was the longest recorded dialogue in the gospels. Many things about his interaction with her were unconventional at the time. Relationships between Jews and Samaritans were so strained that Jews would travel farther to avoid their city. But there was Jesus, alone, talking to the town outcast.

Jesus was intentional about taking the long road to find the woman. Scripture explains that "he *had* to go through Samaria" (John 4:4 NIV, emphasis added). With one little word, the urgency of Jesus' mission leaps off the page. He was on a divine appointment. Waiting at the other end of his journey was a woman with more life wounds than she could count. Even the name of her town, Shechem, meant "a place of burdens." It was a place where God invited the burdened to meet with him.

Jesus hand-delivered an invitation: a decision between two water sources. She could continue to visit the same empty wells to end the drought of her soul, or she could accept his offer of living water. Jesus, the well of life that never runs dry. Her decision was clear. The woman who spent her days avoiding other villagers dropped the water pot and raced back to town. She stood face-to-face with the ones she dreaded and compelled them to meet the man who came for her heart.

There are days when my soul has felt as dry as the dust of Shechem. Like the woman at the well, I have turned to relationships to fill voids. I have run to rest and recreation to feel better, but none of these revived me in the end. Only Jesus has satisfied me.

Jesus crosses mountains to meet you in your place of burdens too. Look to him when you feel empty. Ask Jesus to be near you today. Water from his Spirit saturates the weary soul.

Pause to Reflect

- The woman at the well was depleted because she sought empty sources to meet her needs.
- Jesus is the only one who can saturate the dry, cracked places in our lives.
- The Spirit of God revives our souls as we spend time with him.

Pause to Pray

Lord Jesus, when life feels dry, refresh me with your presence. I open my heart to all you have for me. I ask you to revive me in my time with you. In Jesus' name I pray. Amen.

Breath of Life

The Spirit of God, who raised Jesus from the dead, lives in you. And just as God raised Christ Jesus from the dead, he will give life to your mortal bodies by this same Spirit living within you.

ROMANS 8:11 NLT

A world-renowned escape artist slipped into a human-size fishbowl of water. Faces across the crowd grew wide-eyed as they watched him sink beneath the surface. The timer raced toward sixteen minutes and thirty seconds. Attempting to break the world record for holding one's breath on live television was no small feat. A monitor outside the tank blipped loudly as he fought the racing rhythm of his heart. The faster his heart pumped, the more oxygen his body used. Fear of failure made it beat faster. At eight minutes, he was sure he wouldn't make it out of the tank alive and began planning his exit strategy. He decided to stay underwater and fight the need to breathe.

After ten minutes, his extremities tingled, and blood rushed to his vital organs. Two more minutes and his ears were ringing, and an intense pain shot down his arm. As the clock ticked forward, his stomach began lurching as carbon dioxide poisoned his body. At fourteen minutes, his heart entered ischemia and was no longer able to pump blood adequately. Two minutes later, he was sure of an impending heart attack and began to unstrap from the bowl. Suddenly the escape artist heard screaming and thought he might have suffered cardiac arrest. It took seconds for him to realize that he had just broken the world record holding his breath over seventeen minutes. He thrust his head above water and gasped for air. He was relieved to escape the tank alive.[39]

I can barely hold my breath for over one minute. I know because I just tried. The athletes who compete in static apnea, or breath-holding, accomplish remarkable achievements. However, divers are permitted to rapidly inhale pure oxygen gas (O_2) for thirty minutes before competitions to achieve longer times. The longest non-oxygen-assisted record is eleven minutes and fifty-four seconds. That time is impressive, but it can also be dangerous. While some divers claim they have no side effects from holding their breath, some studies of free divers have suggested brain damage is a likely result.[40]

Life without oxygen is unsustainable. Hypoxemia, or inadequate oxygen in the blood, can be a life-threatening condition. Dizziness, a lack of coordination, and tunnel vision are potential effects of low oxygen levels.[41] Hypoxemia must be addressed quickly. If left untreated it may lead to chronic fatigue, extreme apathy, and even heart failure.

The Spirit of God is like air to our entire being. The word *spirit* in Hebrew and Greek means "breath." Like the body, God breathes his Holy Spirit into our human spirit, which permeates every part of our being. We receive life every time we connect with him. Spiritual growth happens as we draw from the Holy Spirit.

If we go prolonged periods without connecting with God, we might experience effects like spiritual hypoxemia. A lack of vision and direction from the Lord may steer us to wrong choices. We can struggle to have the strength to accomplish God's will. The result may be heart failure or walking away from our relationship with God altogether. When our spirit is active and growing, we can fulfill God's plan for our lives. We have the fortitude, clarity, and wisdom we need to complete our calling.

Like oxygen to our lungs, the Spirit of God gives life to everything he touches. Restoration and rejuvenation are found in him. Physical rest alone does not restore us. No amount of social media, alcohol, or coffee can truly revitalize the soul. In his presence is fullness of joy (Psalm 16:11). Take time to be with him today. We need to breathe deeply God's breath of life.

Pause to Reflect

- God's Spirit is oxygen to the soul.
- Receiving from the Holy Spirit replenishes our being more than any other source.
- The Holy Spirit also gives life to our physical bodies.

Pause to Pray

Lord Holy Spirit, would you come and sit with me? Help me receive from you in my prayer time and in your Word. I open my spirit to you. I ask you to come fill and refresh me with your life-giving presence. In Jesus' name I pray. Amen.

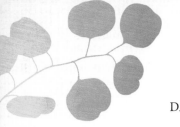

DAY 24

Come Alive

*GOD formed Man out of dirt from the ground
and blew into his nostrils the breath of life.
The Man came alive—a living soul!*

GENESIS 2:5–7 MSG

I pictured the Artist as he surveyed all that was created on the canvas. Admiring eyes carefully scanned the rolling hills and green valleys that formed the horizon. Pinks and oranges glided across the sky and highlighted the clouds. It was captivating yet incomplete. Montages of this magnitude should be shared. A companion would complete the tapestry.

The Artist knelt in the dirt to sculpt a pinnacle piece. Strong hands reached down and gathered ground. I imagine that inspiration illuminated his face as he said to the animals, "This will be a good one. Just watch." Sure, the Artist could have spoken it into existence, but this one was special. Skillful fingers glided across the clay canvas as the mound took shape. The garden animals, with wide eyes, might have nudged closer as the dirt was shaped into a six-foot figure. Each piece was designed with perfect precision. I imagine the Artist dusting off his hands and leaning back to look over the artwork. Throwing his hands in the air, he exclaimed, "Well, what do you think?" The Lord beamed as the animals leaned in with anticipation.

Then God bent down close to the figure. Nose-to-nose with the sculpture, he breathed deeply into the dirt. Air filled the figure to capacity as the clay transformed into flesh. Blood rushed through the veins and warmed the body from head to foot. The man slowly lifted his eyelids. The first thing he saw was the Lord grinning in adoration. Adam smiled back.

Just like the first human, you were created in the image of your Creator. You are as unique as the very first design. Like Adam and Eve were formed in Genesis 2, God molded and shaped your DNA. The Creator desires to breathe into you the same breath that God breathed into the first humans. Still today, each time he comes close, God breathes life.

Breathing is instinctive. The body knows precisely how to contract the lungs to take in oxygen. The spirit is similar in that it understands how to receive from the Lord. As I read the Bible, I can see the winding thread of the breath of God from cover to cover.

The same air that God breathed into Adam is made available to us through Jesus.

In John 20:22, Jesus stepped close to the disciples, breathed on them, and said, "Receive the Holy Spirit" (NLT). The thread continues in Acts chapter 2, when the disciples had gathered in an upper room for prayer. God's power moved on them in the form of a surging wind. I believe that the same type of Holy Spirit infilling can take place when we gather with other believers and seek the Lord. Later we find this same breath referenced in 2 Timothy 3:16. The apostle Paul said that Scripture is given by *divine inspiration*, which in Greek means "God-breathed." Each time we receive the Word of God, we inhale spiritual oxygen. Doing these things intentionally builds up the spirit and grows our connection with God.

I can't say that I am as consistent in connecting with God as I am in breathing. If I pray fifteen to twenty times per minute like I breathe, I might float up to heaven. Even if you aren't conscious of God every minute, you can draw close to him frequently. Prayer time, Scripture reading, and shorter conversations with him throughout the day are all opportunities to receive from the Holy Spirit. If you are not sure what drawing close to God feels like, try taking in a deep breath and filling your lungs completely full. Then take a normal breath. With the same intentionality that you did those lung exercises, you can connect with the Spirit of God. Simple prayer-filled whispers like, *Lord, I love you* or *God, I need you* inch you closer to him. God breathes into the places that feel lifeless within you. The Spirit of God makes you come alive.

Pause to Reflect

- The same life-giving air God breathed into Adam is made available to us through Jesus.
- We take in God's breath of life each time we connect with his Spirit.
- Time in God's presence strengthens our spirit, which grows our ability to receive from him.

Pause to Pray

Heavenly Father, I need you. I ask you to come close today. Breathe life into me. I surrender to you, and I receive from your Spirit. Come alive in me. In Jesus' name I pray. Amen.

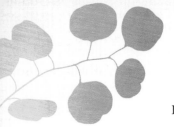

DAY 25

Surplus

*Be filled with the Holy Spirit, singing psalms
and hymns and spiritual songs among yourselves,
and making music to the Lord in your hearts.*
EPHESIANS 5:18–19 NLT

My credit card had just been denied for the first time, and I was mortified. We were trying to buy a suit for BJ for an upcoming wedding. Some miscommunications with our budget, bills, and payday left us caught in the red. I still remember the blatant beep of the credit card machine with each swipe. It was as if it were screaming *Overdraft* repeatedly to those in line behind us. The clerk leaned forward and whispered, "I'm sorry. It says *Insufficient Funds.*" She enunciated each syllable in *insufficient* as if they were individual words. My face flushed. Not having a secondary method of payment, we walked out minus a suit and our pride.

Each of us has a spiritual bank account. What we deposit into it is what is available when we need to make withdrawals. Bishop, a mentor of mine, pointed his finger at me and said, "Kristel, you've got to keep your spiritual bank account in the black." He meant that if I would place consistent deposits from the Holy Spirit into my life, I could draw strength from God when needed. Jesus explained it this way: "Out of the abundance of the heart the mouth speaks" (Matthew 12:34 ESV). What is abundant in our lives comes out when the pressure mounts. As we make daily installments from God into our spirit, we begin to see a surplus. Faith grows. We are able to determine God's will with greater ease. We readily identify direction, instruction, and encouragement from the Holy Spirit. Living by the power of God becomes a possibility.

A younger friend pulled me to the side recently and confessed, "I just feel disconnected from God. I'm trying, but it's like I can't receive from him. I don't know what happened."

I recognized the anguish on her face as one that's been written across my own. As I prayed over her, I felt the Holy Spirit prompt me to say, "God is not mad at you. That's a lie. Your Father is proud of his daughter. God is not distancing himself from you. He desires to be close." Her tense shoulders dropped beneath my hands as peace washed over her mind. Then I looked at her and said, "I can pray these things because I have experienced them too. When I feel far from God, sometimes I think he's mad at me. Condemnation can drive my mind to dark places. I forget that being near to him is as simple as making deposits into my spirit." Relief washed across her face as she embraced God's grace.

Fear keeps me from receiving from God more than anything else. Anxiety seems to create a block in my relationship with the Lord. It feels like God is disappointed in me for being anxious, which slips me further into a fear cycle. When I'm battling fear, I'm not operating in the faith that gives access to the Holy Spirit. That is why Hebrews 11:6 (NLT) says, "It is impossible to please God without faith. Anyone who wants to come to him must believe that God exists and that he rewards those who sincerely seek him." God is not angry at my anxiety, but faith is needed if I desire to connect with him. Faith is the key that activates our spirit.

Each investment into our spirit, whether small or large, adds up. In our intimate times with God in prayer, we receive from the Holy Spirit. Installments of truth from Scripture add to our account. Quick conversations with God during the day become mobile deposits. The result is an overflow of the power of God. When pressures, demands, and priorities press against us, the Spirit of God is what flows out. As we stock our spirit full of the Lord, there's no room for anything fake. Let our spirit not be caught in the red. Abundant life can be found in spiritual surplus.

Pause to Reflect

- Deposits from the Spirit of God keep us spiritually healthy.
- Fear can shut down the faith that gives access to the Holy Spirit.
- When life's pressures press in, whatever we are full of will come out.

Pause to Pray

Lord Holy Spirit, fill me with more of you. Help me to carve out intimate time with you. Be near as I go through my day. Help me receive truth from your Word. I want to live in spiritual surplus so that you flow out of me. In Jesus' name I pray. Amen.

The Focus

*"Vision is the ability to see God's presence,
to perceive God's power,
to focus on God's plan in spite of the obstacles."*[42]
CHARLES R. SWINDOLL

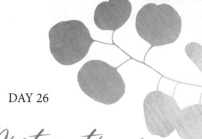

Deny Distractions

Friends, don't get me wrong: By no means do I count myself an expert in all of this, but I've got my eye on the goal, where God is beckoning us onward—to Jesus. I'm off and running, and I'm not turning back.

PHILIPPIANS 3:12–14 MSG

The woman's robe felt weighty in her fragile hands. Her mind wandered to the days when fabrics of brilliant colors filled her wardrobe. With a deep breath, the woman slid the garment around her frail frame. As she tied it closed, a tear tumbled down her cheek. She couldn't remember the last time arms wrapped around her like this linen. The hood sufficiently hid her face in the shadows as she slowly turned toward the door.

The woman's fortune had been wasted on treatments that left her worse in the end. Although her constant bleeding was hidden, everyone knew. She was *unclean*. The invisible label demanded isolation to prevent the spread of the disease. For twelve years, the woman lived separate from society, but she had heard of a man who healed incurable diseases. Chatter of Jesus who confronted customs and settled stigmas had erupted all over the region. The last flicker of faith inside her sparked. Would he dare to touch her? Something inside her said a brush of his clothes would be enough. He *must* be enough.

Outside her home the crowd chanted his name. The woman's eyes locked on his face. Jesus was focused on the local rabbi who appeared distressed. The woman willed her body forward. She ignored the gasps and horrified faces of the crowd as she inched in. Jesus turned around to follow the rabbi. "No, wait," she screamed. With her feet slipping on the stone pavement, the mob pushed her to the ground. She forced herself onto her hands and knees as she tried to catch a glimpse of Jesus through the wall of people. *No more*, the woman thought. *No more sickness. No more loneliness. I must get to him.*

Through the blur of the bodies the woman recognized what looked like the tassels of Jesus' prayer shawl. One by one, she pushed by the people. Her body was weak, but Jesus was within reach. The woman lunged forward and gripped the hem of his linen fabric with all her strength. Power jolted through her body and forced her to her feet. Shaken and trembling, she clutched her stomach. She did not need a doctor to diagnose what had just happened. Jesus had healed her, and she knew it. Wells of gratitude and joy overflowed from the woman's heart. Then Jesus' eyes settled on hers as he reached out his hand. "Daughter, your faith has made you well. Go in peace. Your suffering is over" (Mark 5:34 NLT).

The woman with the issue of blood was never identified in Scripture. Because Jewish law declared her unclean, anyone who brushed against her would also be defiled (Leviticus 15:25–27). She was an outcast to society. After suffering from bleeding for twelve years, she must have been severely anemic. Extreme fatigue, weakness, and dizziness were all likely symptoms she endured, but she was also determined. Her faith forced her toward Jesus. In the midst of her pain, heartache, and loneliness, her attention could not be swayed. This woman positioned herself for a miracle.

Faith not only found her solution, but it also made her famous. Her focus and determination influenced others in her region. People from neighboring villages begged to touch the hem of Jesus' shawl and were healed. Jesus restored her health, reputation, and likely her relationships. To everyone else the woman was nameless, but to Jesus she was *daughter*.

I can't say that faith will put you in a spotlight, but I will promise that it grabs God's attention. Deny the distractions and lock eyes with Jesus today. Within him is all the power for your problems, and his hand is extended toward you.

Pause to Reflect

- Distractions try to drag our attention away from Jesus.
- We don't ignore problems and pain, but we process them through our relationship with God.
- The Lord notices uncommon faith.

Pause to Pray

Heavenly Father, when distractions come at me like giants, I turn my attention to your face. You are more important than all my problems. I choose to place struggle and pain at your feet today and set my eyes on you. In Jesus' name I pray. Amen.

Weightless

Those who wait upon GOD get fresh strength. They spread their wings and soar like eagles, They run and don't get tired, they walk and don't lag behind.
ISAIAH 40:27–37 MSG

Baeksul perched on her handler's hand, spread her eight-foot wings, and leapt to take flight. Then she pulled back and withdrew her instincts. Instead of gliding across the sky, she dropped to the ground. Baeksul was a bald eagle, but she didn't know it. This eagle walked like a human everywhere she went. Her soar was reduced to a saunter on feet that weren't meant for the ground. When her trainers presented an opportunity for her to hunt, Baeksul preferred to socialize with humans. Her razor-sharp talons designed to imprison prey gently held her handler's bare arm instead. Live fish swimming in her bowl frightened and repulsed her instead of triggering fierce predatory instincts. Baeksul was both majestic and mighty, and everyone recognized it…except her.

Baeksul didn't know that her wings could carry her higher than the clouds. Her eyes were fit to scan the ground from over three miles high. Baeksul's talons were designed to drag away prey heavier than half her body weight. Her vision was three times sharper than her handlers' sight. Baeksul could track another eagle in the sky from fifty miles away. She was uniquely designed to soar, hunt, and subdue, but Baeksul had an identity crisis. Because she had lived with humans since infancy, Baeksul did not know how to be an eagle.[43]

For far too long, many of us have pecked the dirt like chickens instead of ascending like eagles. We were called to soar with God, but our feet have often been anchored to the ground by anxieties. The worries of life keep our wings crowded at our sides instead of fit for flight. We were designed to be victorious. Distracted and distressed by problems on the ground, we miss opportunities to rise with God. When our eyes are cast down and our feet are dragging the ground, the Lord calls us higher. *Come up here with me and see what I see*, God whispers his invitation. *And I'll show you how to soar.*

My friend's hunger for God stirred great conversation on the phone recently. Question after question, the Holy Spirit guided our discussion. Right before ending the call, I heard these words tumble from my lips, "Oh, real quick before we go…I feel like God gave me a verse for you." I read off the familiar passage from Isaiah, "But those who trust in the Lord will find new strength. They will soar high on wings like eagles. They will run and not grow weary. They will walk and not faint" (Isaiah 40:31 NLT). She listened intently on the other end. "But I noticed something cool this time that I hadn't seen when reading this verse before," I continued. "As I read, I wondered what it means to 'trust in the Lord.' So I looked up *trust* in Hebrew," I explained. "*Qâvâh, Kaw-vaw,* I think is how you say it. Anyway, it means 'to entwine,' which I thought was beautiful. Those who entwine themselves together with the Lord will rise up like eagles." I paused my Bible-nerd monologue. She was silent on the other end. As the quiet became uncomfortable, she finally spoke up. My friend explained that God had given her a special word for the year. It was a message she clung to when complications came her way. Her word from the Lord was *qâvâh,* "to entwine." She had the exact word in Hebrew and the definition documented in her journal long before our conversation that day. We praised the Lord for his goodness and determined to mesh our hearts together with God's in prayer.

As we entangle our hearts with the Lord's, we see with fresh eyes. Anxiety, worry, and stress no longer have a hold on us as we rise higher with God. In our prayer time we gain a heavenly vantage point for our problems here on earth. God establishes our identity, lifts our weights, and cuts our anchors.

Pause to Reflect

- God did not design us to be distracted and weighted by the problems in life.
- As our hearts become one with the Lord's in prayer, we soar above stressful situations.
- In God's presence we gain insight into our difficulties on the ground.

Pause to Pray

Lord, help me entwine my heart with yours in prayer. When I feel weighted by worries, show me what you see. Give me your heavenly viewpoint. I don't want anxieties to hold me to the ground any longer. I want to soar with you. In Jesus' name I pray. Amen.

Worthy

You protect me with your saving shield.
You support me with your right hand.
You have stooped to make me great.

PSALM 18:35 NCV

*I*mpostor. The label echoed in Pauline's mind night and day. Though she was a successful graduate student at a prestigious university, Pauline feared that she was one test short of failure.[44] Her friends grew annoyed by her anxieties. Pauline concealed her insecurity under a mask of confidence. Upon completion of her doctoral degree, Dr. Pauline Clance taught at a respected liberal arts university. Many of her students expressed the same feelings she struggled with in graduate school. One young man confided in her, saying, "I feel like an impostor here with all these really bright people." [45] Dr. Clance and her colleague, Dr. Suzanne Imes, later defined this feeling of unworthiness as the impostor syndrome.

Sadly, the worst sufferers of impostor syndrome are often the highest performers. Every year, two-thirds of Stanford Business School students think their acceptance came from an admissions board error. When the impostor syndrome is discussed at Harvard or MIT, the room drops to silence.[46] Even Albert Einstein once shared with a friend, "The exaggerated esteem in which my lifework is held makes me very ill at ease. I feel compelled to think of myself as an involuntary swindler." [47] Harvard grad Natalie Portman[48] and Nobel Laureate Maya Angelou[49] both admitted to struggling with these same fears. Some of the world's brightest minds have silently screamed, *Impostor!*

As I was studying this impostor phenomenon, I scanned mindlessly through another psychology article. I scrolled until one paragraph halted my cursor. This particular author sealed her research with an unconventional statement of grace:

> At the end of the day, remember this: You are here for a reason. In this job, your business, your life, you are worthy. You are better than you think you are. You are smarter than you think you are. You know more than you give yourself credit for. Remember that. And remind yourself as often as you need to.[50]

Impostor has invaded my mind at times too. *What if they find out I'm not really as close to God as they think? What if I pray and it all falls apart?* Sometimes I feel like a fraud as I walk into church with a big smile and a heart full of pain. There are mornings when my fears of failure fill my time with God and push out the encouragement of the Holy Spirit. I have felt like God was ready to hurl a lightning bolt at me for my shortcomings. (By the way, God doesn't throw lightning bolts. That's Zeus.) If I'm honest, I have felt insecure while writing these pages to you.

Feelings of inferiority are partially correct. You and I are not enough on our own. Jesus, however, exceeds all expectations and qualifications. He is more than enough. Yet in his superiority, he chose to exchange his perfect life for ours. Jesus didn't come only for the Sunday morning, Instagram-filtered, perfectly dressed version of us. No, he got his hands dirty with our darkest days. Scripture says that while we were still sinners, Jesus died for you and me (Romans 5:8). The messed-up, fed-up, broken-up versions of ourselves were on his mind while on the cross. And he has shown up for us every day since. Jesus redeems what has been damaged and makes it better than brand new.

Friend, you are chosen by God. The creator of the universe treasures you. The Holy Spirit dwells inside you. He has set a path before your feet and provides what you need for the journey. Show up and shine today. Jesus *in you* is more than enough.

Pause to Reflect

- Some of the most accomplished people in the world have often felt like a fraud.
- We are incomplete and insufficient on our own.
- Jesus demonstrated our value to God by exchanging his life for ours on the cross.

Pause to Pray

Father, sometimes I don't feel like much. There are days when it seems that people will think I'm an impostor. But God, you are everything. Fill my life with your presence and power. Remind me that you're near when I feel like I'm failing. Because of you, I am enough. In Jesus' name I pray. Amen.

Eye Adjustment

"The eyes of the LORD search the whole earth
in order to strengthen those whose hearts
are fully committed to him."

2 CHRONICLES 16:9 NLT

Melissa wrung her tissue between her fingers. The hospital room felt small as I watched worry wash over her face. Soon her body would be so sore that it would hurt to wipe tears from her cheeks. Side-effects like unforgiving fatigue and relentless nausea were tugging at her attention. "Hey," I said, as I set my fears aside. "You're almost done. Just one more treatment." My encouragement was sincere yet unsure. Joining hands, we prayed through a list of healing Scriptures. We asked God that the medicine would do its job and nothing else.

The nurse interrupted as she hung multiple bags from the IV pole. "Oh, sorry. Keep praying. Every little bit helps." She hummed as she connected the tubes and thumped the dripping IV. "Ok, your chemo cocktail is going strong." Melissa and I shot an annoyed look at each other and flipped on the TV to watch *Fixer Upper*. Melissa drew up her blanket and drifted to sleep. My best friend and I had supported each other through many things over the years, but cancer was a first.

A few days later, I juggled an armful of herbal supplements as I squeezed quietly through Melissa's door. My normally busy-bee friend was curled on the couch, skin pale and head covered for warmth. She squeaked out a quiet, "Hi," and went back to writing something.

"What on earth are you working on?" I had expected her to be asleep.

Her response was feeble yet determined. "I've been writing letters of encouragement to ladies at church."

"Seriously? Can't you just take a nap?" I tried not to roll my eyes, but I think I failed.

She muttered, "Can't sleep. Might as well do something while I'm lying here."

One by one, Melissa prayed over each letter and let God speak through her words. As I walked out of the house that day, the Holy Spirit checked my heart. How would I react if our roles were switched? I knew that I would have binge-watched HGTV and Food Network.

My encouraging postcards would have been addressed to myself. I realized I needed to reframe my focus.

Melissa's eyes stayed focused on hope through countless hospital visits. Phrases like "This too shall pass" and "This is not my forever" consistently fell from her lips. When side-effects and insomnia struck at night, Melissa lay in bed praying for people. God's faithfulness was as secure on her darkest days as her brightest. Scripture promises that the Lord is closest when we are the most vulnerable (Psalm 34:18). God's strength, stability, and the sureness of his Word were evident while I walked with Melissa through cancer. Sickness didn't cancel her calling. Cancer didn't pry away her purpose. She became even more intentional about genuinely seeing people. Melissa bravely chose to see her story in the breadth of God's goodness instead of the misery of the moment.

When life is stormy and my anchors are slipping, I am tempted to turn my attention on myself. The war within my mind tries to justify my feelings. The longer I remain in this state, the more my thoughts spiral out of control. When I manage to flip my focus outward onto others, my troubles seem to shrink. I dare to pray for people in the grocery store and listen with compassion instead of irritation. I can look the cashier in the eye and respond with a smile. It's not that I ignore my needs or emotions, which is also unhealthy. But dilemmas no longer get to stand in the spotlight of my mind. The Holy Spirit gets center stage.

Scripture says that the Lord's eyes search the earth looking to strengthen those he loves. We are most like him when we genuinely see the souls circling our lives. Melissa taught me that people are eternal, but problems are not.

Pause to Reflect

- Choose to give your greatest attention to God's truths instead of troubles.
- Our mental state is healthier when we are giving.
- A heavenly viewpoint is focused on empathetically caring for others.

Pause to Pray

Lord, help me when my eyes wander from your promises and onto my problems. Draw my attention to those who need encouragement. Show me how to bless others instead of dwelling in depression or fear. I trust you with all my problems. I know you care about them. Help me see people the way you do. In Jesus' name. Amen.

Focus on Truth

*Since you have been raised to new life with Christ,
set your sights on the realities of heaven, where Christ
sits in the place of honor at God's right hand.*
COLOSSIANS 3:1 NLT

Joshua wiped the dirt and sweat from his brow. His hands shook from the back of the ranks as he counted his men for the third time. Spearmen, archers, and swordsmen stood motionless in anticipation of attack. Joshua gripped his sword closer to his side, as the tension thickened like the desert dust beneath his feet. Glaring images of yesterday's invasion plagued his thoughts. The bodies of the children and elders pierced with Amalekite arrows flashed across his mind. Joshua sighed and wondered, *Where is Moses?* His eyes bounced upon the hilltop in search of their leader and then on the horizon in apprehension of the enemy. It was then he heard hooves in the distance.

Amalekite camels became visible as they neared for battle. "Steady!" Joshua yelled firmly over his restless men. Suddenly the shadows of three figures blocked the sun. The Israelites instantly recognized Moses, Hur, and Aaron. Moses fiercely stepped forward and thrust his shepherd's staff high in the air. The Israelite camp broke out in a warrior roar. Joshua's mind flashed to the carvings etched into the wood of Moses' staff. He remembered running his fingers over the lines of each picture. As he had felt their ridges, he recalled each victory God had won for his people. With it raised high over the battlefield, faith swelled from the depths of Joshua's heart.

As the enemy lunged forward, the Israelite men dug their heels into the dirt. With one look at Moses' staff, they planted their feet, steadied their swords, and drew their bows. The two camps clashed in an array of commotion. Iron, flesh, and fear melted together across the battlefield. Each time the Israelite men looked up from their fight toward the staff, faith propelled them forward.

Moses' eighty-year-old frame grew weary as the day stretched on. Each time he lowered the staff, Joshua's men lost focus and faltered. Staggering back, they grew weak and fatigued. Aaron and Hur quickly retrieved a rock for Moses to sit on as they propped up his arms. With the staff back in its place faith conquered the fear in the hearts of the men. And after a long Israelite resistance, the Amalekites finally turned in retreat. The entire camp raised their weapons. They lifted voices in praise to God as Moses held his staff high over the sunset desert. This rabble group of former slaves just won their very first fight (Exodus 17:8–16).

You may feel like you're on the frontlines of a battle today. When you hear lies coming against you, recognize that is not the time to shrink back. Set your sights on the truth in God's word. As the Israelites focused on Moses' staff, they undoubtedly remembered when he raised it over the Red Sea and they walked through on dry ground. They probably remembered when Moses had struck a rock and water had burst forth in the middle of a desert. The staff must have brought them comfort as it reminded them of the goodness of God.

As I'm writing to you, my eyes land on a Word Board hanging above the desk. Pinned all over it are tiny Scripture promises, reminders of God's grace during tough times. I have prayed these verses over my family, finances, and ministry during difficult circumstances. When in the thick of battle, coming out of one, or heading into one, we need to be filled with the Word of God. What we fill ourselves with when all is calm is what will come out when the battle is hot.

Pause to Reflect

- When a crisis comes, remember the good things God has done.
- Turn to the truth of God's Word when lies are flying like arrows.
- Fill yourself with Scripture during easy seasons so you have something to draw from when times are tough.

Pause to Pray

Lord Holy Spirit, teach me your Word. Overflow my spirit with your life-giving truth. Lord, I need your Word on good days as much as bad ones. Write Scripture all over my heart. Guide me in understanding the Bible. Then the power of your promises will be there when I need them most. In Jesus' name I pray. Amen.

The Calling

*"The two most important days in your life are the day
you are born and the day you find out why."*
UNKNOWN

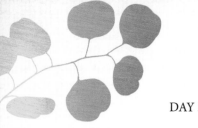

DAY 31

Defrost Your Dreams

"I am God.
At the right time I'll make it happen."
ISAIAH 60:8–22 MSG

Conflict stirred within as I attempted to blend into the audience. The secret struggles in my heart felt exposed as the conference speaker addressed the crowd. Midway through the sermon, she declared, "There are frozen callings in this congregation." The weight of that statement hit my spirit like bricks. *No, Lord*, I whispered. *I can't hope any longer for things that never come to pass.* God spoke softly in return, *I will be with you. It's time to take your calling off the shelf.*

Two years prior I had packed away my ministry dreams. Ambitions of public speaking, teaching the Bible, and writing books drove me to push past God's timing. I felt ready to walk into my purpose, but the doors of opportunity were locked. There were no invitations for me to speak, and the remains of a manuscript sat on my hard drive. The verse "Hope deferred makes the heart sick" in Proverbs 13:12 (NIV) explained my feelings. Frustrated and wounded by the appearance of a missed calling, I boxed up the pain in my heart.

From my chair at the conference, I felt the Lord prompt me to respond for prayer. I watched others make their way to the front. It was a short distance to where they were standing, but it felt like a mile in my heart. I sat in my seat and wrestled between responding to God and fear of failure. The desire to follow God finally outweighed my hurt, and I rose from the chair. Leery of trusting my grief to the Father, I knelt and prayed, *You're going to have to do it. I can't make things happen on my own.* The pain poured out as tender tears dripped to the carpet. *Oh good. We can start then*, I sensed the Lord respond with open arms. His gentle grace washed over my wounds. It was time to defrost my dreams.

Book deals and speaking engagements didn't flood my inbox. However, preparation for fulfilling my purpose started immediately. The next day of the conference, I met a writing coach who facilitated my journey as an emerging author. Within a short amount of time, God created connections with seasoned ministers who invested in my calling. Puzzle pieces in my life began to shift. BJ took a work-from-home job that allowed for travel flexibility. Other schedule requirements disappeared, which permitted more time to write and speak. God opened doors and steadied my steps as I gripped his hand in obedience.

Years later, I'm drinking a cup of coffee as I write to you. And I hope that you know the freedom and fulfillment of walking hand in hand with God. There might be a yearning in your heart to understand your purpose. Maybe there is a void inside that longs to be filled with accomplished dreams. I hope you hear that it's time to call out your calling.

With anxious eyes, others often ask me, "How do I find God's plan for my life?" We all want to know our place. Discovering purpose is a universal need, but it's important to remember that our primary role on earth is to love God. Our deepest need is to know him and allow the Holy Spirit access to the private places of our hearts. As we are with the Lord in prayer and in his Word, the Spirit of God reveals our next step. Assignments are handed out through an intimate relationship with Jesus. But instead of asking the big question, *What is my calling?* Try asking, *God, what are you calling me to do right now?* Obedience to the Lord in this season gives us what is needed for the next one. Whenever we submit to God, we're successful. Accomplished dreams are like sunshine to a weary soul.

Pause to Reflect

- It is time to defrost frozen dreams.
- Our calling is revealed through intimate time with Jesus.
- Instead of asking God for the whole plan, try asking him for your next steps.

Pause to Pray

Lord, I want your will to be done in me. I desire a life that has meaning and impact. My purpose is first to love you, but I sense that there is more. I ask you to reveal what you are calling me to do in this season. I trust you with my dreams, Lord. In Jesus' name. Amen.

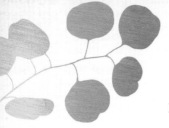

Power Within

> *"Before I shaped you in the womb,*
> *I knew all about you.*
> *Before you saw the light of day,*
> *I had holy plans for you."*
> JEREMIAH 1:5 MSG

The tale of two royal sisters, Elsa and Anna, played out in the dark theater as I watched *Frozen* with my girls. Turmoil created by Elsa's uncontrollable magic ice powers kept us glued to the screen. The story begins as the sisters play in the palace. The younger Anna urges Elsa to create an enchanted snow land inside the ballroom. Flicking her fingers, Elsa paints frozen hills across the floor. As Anna sprints across the snow, an accidental ray of ice hits her head and knocks her unconscious. Elsa screams for her parents as the family fears for Anna's life.

Anna makes a full recovery, but not Elsa. Petrified of her power, she locks herself away in her room. As Elsa's anxiety grows, the ice involuntarily erupts from her fingertips. The kingdom, palace, and especially Anna grow dreary in Elsa's absence.

Years passed, and the girls remained separated by walls and ice. When Elsa turns eighteen, it is time for her to assume the throne of Arendelle as queen. The elaborate Coronation Celebration hosts dignitaries from kingdoms near and far. One handsome guest, Prince Hans, takes a romantic interest in Anna although they just met. The younger sister approaches the queen to ask her blessing on her marriage to Hans, but Elsa refuses their request, and an argument explodes between Anna and Elsa.

"All you know is how to shut people out," Anna hurls angrily at her sister.

"Enough," Elsa warns, but Anna presses harder. "I said enough!" Elsa exclaims as she throws her arms, sending unintentional daggers of ice toward Anna. Elsa's fear finally erupts and covers all of Arendelle in inches of thick snow and ice. In an instant, the warmth of spring is exchanged for a harsh winter as Elsa retreats farther from the people. In a later scene, Anna finds Elsa deep in the woods in a palace of ice. She tiptoes inside, intent on convincing Elsa to save Arendelle from the throes of the unexpected winter. Another argument ensues, and in this instance, Elsa's outburst of ice accidentally hits Anna in her heart. This time, the wound may be fatal. Then begins the frantic quest to save Arendelle, and now Anna, from Elsa's misplaced powers.

At the end of the film, all of Arendelle is now encased in a blizzard. Anna is nearly frozen as she approaches death. She squints to see Elsa facedown in despair with Hans approaching behind. Instead of helping Elsa, Hans reaches across his hip and draws his sword. Anna rushes toward her sister as Hans raises his weapon. He thrusts it down. A fully frozen Anna falls beneath the steel, shatters the blade, and saves the queen. Elsa's greatest fears have now come to pass. She has killed her only sister and beloved kingdom. Elsa pours out her devastation on her sister's chest, and Anna's body slowly begins to warm. Heat from the heart crosses her entire body, bringing Anna back to life. The sisters stare at each other and realize in unison, "Love thaws a frozen heart." Now using love instead of fear, Elsa defrosts all of Arendelle. The splendor of spring and her place on the throne of the kingdom are rightfully restored.[51]

In the story of *Frozen*, Elsa was born with power inside her. The more she ran from it, the unhappier she became. No amount of hiding could mask who she was destined to become. By embracing her identity, she was able to tap in to the powers within. While not fairy-tale, magic ice powers, you, too, have gifts God has stored on the inside of you. Do you feel them? Do you know what they are? Possibly, like me, you have buried them in hurt. Or maybe, like Elsa, you have hidden your gifts in fear. Or possibly, like Anna, you have whirled through life unaware of their existence. Behind whichever door you find yourself, love is the key that unlocks your calling. Falling in love with Jesus and following him with your life uncovers your purpose. Love for God's people causes you to release hidden gifts into a world that needs them. And love thaws frozen hearts.

Pause to Reflect

- Falling in love with Jesus reveals your calling.
- The world needs the gifts God placed inside you.
- Love for God's people will prompt you to walk in your purpose.

Pause to Pray

Father, I want to fall more in love with you every day. I also ask for a greater love for your people. You sacrificed your life for them. Show me how I can better serve people. In Jesus' name I pray. Amen.

Broken Vessels

*Every believer has received grace gifts,
so use them to serve one another
as faithful stewards of the many-colored
tapestry of God's grace.*
1 PETER 4:10–11 TPT

Tears streamed down my cheeks as I stared at the computer screen. In a few weeks, I would be teaching a group the online spiritual gifts class I was taking. Yet, I was unsure if God was happy with me. *Why did you make me this way, Lord?* I prayed silently. Condemnation over my shortcomings came at me like arrows. *You're too bossy*, the shots screamed past my ears. *You just hurt people*, another one buzzed over-head. How could God use me with all these faults? I wondered if the Lord would lessen my calling when I lose my temper with my kids, show up late to meet-ings, or mistreat my husband. I tried to push back destructive thoughts when a Scripture verse came up on my screen. First Peter 4:10 said, "God has given each of you a gift from his great variety of spiritual gifts. Use them well to serve one another" (NLT). With a sigh of relief, it sank in that each of you includes me.

I wiped my cheeks, slid open my Bible, and sought answers for my anxieties. In my search, I discovered that the Greek word for "gifts" is charisma. I continued to read and found that the root of *charisma* is *charis*, which translated into English is "grace." The substance of the gifts God placed inside me is his grace. When I accept my callings and operate in them, God's grace flows from me to other people. The argument that I wasn't good enough began to unravel. The more I leaned in and listened to God, I realized that he fashioned my personality around my purpose. God wanted to redeem my identity, wrap it in his love, and use it for his glory. God planted his grace in my DNA with the intention to partner with me to dispense it to the world.

A fallible person can be found on nearly every page of the Bible. The apostle Peter might stand out among the rest. He once rebuked Jesus for prophesying the Messiah's death on the cross. I couldn't imagine correcting the Christ. When situations called for surrender, Peter wanted to draw swords. I wondered how often Jesus rolled his eyes at Peter's impulses. Sparks flew later in Acts when the apostle Paul openly rebuked Peter for hypocrisy in ministry. Peter's errors went as far as denying Christ while the Savior was on his way to the cross. Throughout the New Testament, we watch God repeatedly redeem Peter's faults. Through all his shortcomings, he was still chosen to lead the church. Peter's ministry opened Christianity to the rest of the world. The Spirit of God flowed from him so freely that Peter's shadow healed the sick. He later wrote today's key verse encouraging us to use our gifts to serve one another even if we have a few flaws along the way.

Friend, God placed grace-gifts inside you too. These gifts are often identified as things that feel challenging to others but seem simple to you. God molded and shaped your character to fit your calling. Your personality may not be perfect, but spiritual gifts are not negated by faults. God wants to redeem your weaknesses. Know the next time you care for the neighbor's children, speak love to the hurting, or pay it forward at the drive-through, you are giving away grace. Forsake the shadows and shine bright. Don't allow flaws to stop you from using the gifts inside you. God's grace is often dispensed to the world through broken vessels.

Pause to Reflect

- Spiritual gifts are identified as things that are difficult for others but simple to you.
- Personal faults do not disqualify our calling.
- God's grace flows through our gifts.

Pause to Pray

Lord, I want to serve you with all that I have. I am imperfect, but I know that you are shaping me to be more like you. I ask you to help me use the gifts you have placed inside me. Let your grace flow through me to the world. In Jesus' name I pray. Amen.

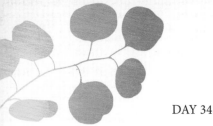

Pour Out

"'Not by might, nor by power, but by My Spirit [of whom the oil is a symbol],' says the Lord of hosts."
ZECHARIAH 4:6 AMP

I imagined that the widow opened heavy eyelids as morning light filtered into her empty home. She hoped it was a bad dream, but the room looked the same. Hollow and dry like her heart. Yesterday she sold everything except her last flask of olive oil in the corner. She sat up on the floor and stared at her two sons sleeping on the other side of the room. Nausea swept over as she mentally prepared for the day.

A bang at the door demanded her attention. Her voice sounded weak as she responded, "Yes? Can I help you?"

The man on the other side shouted, "Time's up. I've come to collect your husband's debt."

She interrupted, "Oh yes, I have one more deal to make. I will have the full amount tomorrow," even though she doubted her words.

The man pointed behind her and said, "If you don't have it in the morning, I'm taking those boys with me!"

The widow slammed the door shut and commanded, "Boys, get up. We're going to see the prophet."

Across town the woman pounded on Elisha's door. There was no time for pleasantries. "How can I help you?" Elisha asked.

With arms waving, she began, "My husband who served you is dead…but now a creditor has come, threatening to take my two sons as slaves."

Unemotional, he asked, "What's in your house?"

The woman hung her head, "Nothing except a flask of olive oil."

Elisha peered at the woman and said, "Borrow as many empty jars as you can from your friends and neighbors. Then go into your house with your sons and shut the door behind you. Pour olive oil from your flask into the jars, setting each one aside when it is filled." The woman stared as Elisha closed the door behind him.

The widow directed her sons, "Ask all the neighbors for jars. Explain nothing of our situation. Leave no house behind."

Back in her empty home the widow picked up her flask of olive oil. Her son put the first empty vessel in front of her. The widow sighed deeply, lifted the jug, and trickled oil into the empty vessel. "Mom," the son gripped her shoulder in amazement. The jar was full. Now two containers of olive oil sat on the counter.

The widow cried, "Hurry! Bring me every flask you can find!" The two boys filled the room with empty jars, and the woman laughed as she kept pouring. One by one, their jug of oil turned into twenty, then fifty, and finally more than one hundred bottles. The golden-colored oil kept flowing until the last flask was filled.[52]

How often do we feel barren and bankrupt like the widow? Sometimes it seems that there is nothing unique about us that God can use. The Lord replies to our self-doubt, *What's that?* and points out the potential we've never considered. God placed ministry inside of every person. Your place to serve may be from a microphone to many people, or it may be hugging a hurting coworker. It may be to preach a sermon or to open a door for a neighbor. Whatever your hand finds to do for God, do so with all your heart.

Give your *nothing* to the Lord and watch what he'll do with it. Hand him your time, talent, and treasure. Open your hands and offer to the Father what little you think you have. Remember that we don't serve the Lord in our own power and strength but through the Spirit of God. If you'll pour, he'll provide. Those who give generously are the first to receive in return. What do you have in your *house* that God can use?

Pause to Reflect

- God will take your nothing and turn it into something miraculous.
- Pour out your service to the Lord when you feel ordinary and empty.
- We don't serve God in our own strength but through the power of his Spirit.

Pause to Pray

Heavenly Father, I present my heart in obedience to you when I feel that I have nothing of value to offer. Show me what you want me to do. Place people in my path that I can bless and encourage. Provide the words to say and the strength to serve. In Jesus' name I pray. Amen.

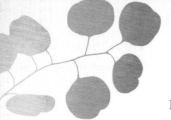

Full Term

The confidence of my calling enables me to overcome every difficulty without shame, for I have an intimate revelation of this God. And my faith in him convinces me that he is more than able to keep all that I've placed in his hands safe and secure until the fullness of his appearing.

2 TIMOTHY 1:12 TPT

Lizzy panicked as she called Manny for the eighth time from the doctor's office. Pregnant with her first baby, she had started to bleed earlier that morning. The doctor had left the room and confirmed Lizzy's fear: the baby no longer had a heartbeat. In ten minutes, her hopes were hushed by a silent ultrasound screen. Now she sat on the examining table, phone in hand and alone. The baby was gone.

Like Lizzy, over 20 percent of pregnant women miscarry. I am one of those, and possibly you are too. I often hold hands and pray with people who experience the heartache of staring at a silent screen. During future pregnancies, these precious ladies are sometimes racked with the fear of losing another child. The joy of awaiting the arrival of their miracle is washed away by worry. Past experience robs them of the wonder found in their season of waiting.

Many women fear miscarrying spiritually too. There are hopes and dreams that the Lord implanted into our souls. But what if we lose them? What if their destinies are cut short? I, too, have lamented over possibly losing my purpose. As I sat across the table from a mentor of mine, Dr. Tracey Mitchell, she offered an explanation for my anxiety. "Women often fear that they will miscarry their calling." My insides relaxed as she spoke. I knew she was right. At that moment I decided to trust God's timing and embrace grace for my life.

The Scriptures are filled with people who failed before they ever succeeded. Sarah dismissed the idea that God would give her a child but later gave birth to her firstborn son. Moses was called by God to bring his people out of captivity. Before becoming a deliverer, he committed murder. Forty years later, he was given a second opportunity and led 2.5 million people to freedom. The apostle Paul persecuted Christians before he encountered Jesus. God later used Paul to spread the gospel to two continents and write two-thirds of the New Testament. Despite their failures,

God secured their assignments until their maturity matched their purpose. God protected their promise until it was time to be delivered.

Waiting seasons are meant for preparation. God is not being cruel when he withholds a calling. He is equipping you to carry your promise to full term. The words of the apostle Paul offer encouragement in the waiting, "The confidence of my calling enables me to overcome every difficulty...And my faith in him convinces me that he is more than able to keep all that I've placed in his hands safe and secure." Speaker and author, Havilah Cunnington, brings peace to distant dreams, "It's in knowing we have a God who sees the whole picture and is making all things work together, that we can relax."[53] Trust in God when your dreams seem delayed. The one who placed them inside you knows the proper time for fulfillment. Reject the lies that say you will lose your promise while you're waiting.

Fear of failure, regret of lost time, and shame of sin all want to cancel our callings. If we're not careful, we'll believe their lies. They sell slander such as *You're not good enough for this, You've missed your opportunity*, and *You're going to have to earn forgiveness first*. Friend, God is too big to let you fail. He is the author of time and redeems it in your favor. There is no magnitude of sin that measures up to God's grace. Those lies are not for you. All of God's goodness is made available on your behalf. The Lord can keep the dreams hidden inside of you safe from harm. Stay by Jesus, and he'll deliver you to your destiny.

Pause to Reflect

- God has dreams hidden inside you.
- The Lord is powerful enough to protect your purpose.
- Seek God in your season of waiting.

Pause to Pray

Lord, help me when I feel I've lost my calling. I surrender my faults and failures to you. I trust you to protect the secret dreams inside me. Guard them until your appropriate time. I want to walk hand in hand with you as you guide my steps. In Jesus' name I pray. Amen.

The Journey

*"The feeling remains that God
is on the journey, too."*
TERESA OF ÁVILA

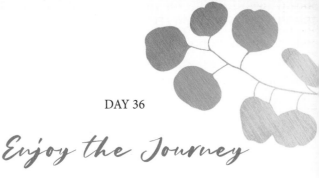

Enjoy the Journey

*I believe that I shall look
upon the goodness of the LORD
in the land of the living!*
PSALM 27:13 ESV

Smoke billows into the bedroom as Jack hands his teenage son a towel. Jack says to Randall, "Towel goes under the door the second it closes. If I'm not back in three minutes, you take your mother out that window." Jack glances at his wife, Rebecca, then he points his finger at Randall, "If she won't go, you drag her out." Then he rushes through the fire to his teen daughter's bedroom.

BJ and I tensed on the couch as we watched the much-anticipated episode of *This Is Us*. On the screen, Jack bursts through Kate's door. He tries to calm his daughter, "We're just going across the hall. It's too high to get down from over here. Ready?" Jack searches for extra protection from the fire, then he strips the mattress and uses it as a shield. He and Kate edge between the flames and the wall with the mattress sheltering them. They throw themselves into the other bedroom. One by one, Jack slides the family down the roof outside to safety. As he is about to climb down, the dog barks. "I think I can get to him," Jack yells and rushes back into the house. Rebecca, Kate, and Randall scream from the street as flames erupt in the windows.

Before the fire, the Pearsons were preparing their annual family Super Bowl party. Chili simmered in the slow cooker. The event was ready, but none of the kids were home. All three had gone to other parties. Jack and Rebecca remained behind wrestling with the transition into raising adults. They fell asleep watching the game.

Jack woke up to the sound of Randall and Kate coming home, but the third of the teens, Kevin, stayed with a friend. Jack cleaned the kitchen from the uneventful party. He glanced at the kid's growth chart etched on the wall while sweeping the floor. Jack sighed and headed to bed. As he climbed the stairs, the light on the slow cooker flickered back on. A spark shot out from the knob, catching the curtains on fire. Later that night at the hospital, Jack suffered a heart attack from smoke inhalation and died.[54]

In *This Is Us*, Jack was not a perfect man, but he loved well. He often viewed life through a lens as he captured meaningful moments of his family. At the end of the fateful night of the fire, he went to bed thinking ahead to tomorrow. Jack didn't know that tomorrow wouldn't come. His life wasn't without hardships, but he died having enjoyed the journey.

Sometimes I have trouble seeing the goodness of God surrounding me. When I'm able to shift my perspective, I recognize that life's little annoyances are often attached to blessings. The dishes that overflow the sink are signs of meals with family and friends. Piles of dirty laundry are left behind by the loved ones who live in them. Dirt on the floor from the dog is—no, that's just irritating. Fleeting moments of joy become passing memories when I forget to hang on to them. For me, the thing that makes me the most forgetful is fear.

Fear forces us to live in the *what if* of the future while robbing the joy in the present. Worries steal the peace that the Lord richly provides. Fear is disarmed of its power when we trust that God is entirely good and working on our behalf. There are over seven thousand promises in Scripture from the Father to his children. The Bible assures that the Lord provides for our needs (Philippians 4:13). We don't have to worry because the Holy Spirit turns every situation for our benefit (Romans 8:28). Fear is expelled from our hearts as we receive God's love (1 John 4:4). Peace is found in the present when we recognize the goodness of God in our midst. Joy overflows as we look past the problems to the blessings of God (Hebrews 12:2).

Today, take a moment to watch the trees sway beneath the sky. Count the freckles on your kids' faces. Walk into work aware that the Lord is with you. Enjoy your journey. The road may have some deep holes and sharp turns, but it is paved with the goodness of God.

Pause to Reflect

- Fear robs the peace and joy that Jesus provides.
- A rich life is lived in remembering the Lord's faithfulness.
- We can have joy in trials as we focus on the promises of God.

Pause to Pray

Heavenly Father, I want to enjoy the life you've given me. Help me see your blessings all around. I will remember your goodness when troubles come. You walk beside me on the path of life. In Jesus' name I pray. Amen.

Know God's Will

Trust in the LORD with all your heart;
do not depend on your own understanding.
Seek his will in all you do,
and he will show you which path to take.

PROVERBS 3:5–6 NLT

Like most soon-to-be newlyweds, BJ and I faced one million uneasy decisions. Where would we work in a new city? Where would we live? Where would we go to church? The choices made us feel as if we were standing in tall grass with no clearly defined paths. Fear of wrong decisions made our feet heavy. We prayed, "Lord, we're not sure if these plans are your will or not, but we're trusting you to lead us." The next steps felt more like walking on shaky sand than solid faith. BJ accepted an entry-level position in his industry. While finishing college, I secured a spot as a server at a restaurant. A cramped and outdated apartment became our first home. We longed for an audible voice from the Lord that declared, *Go ye this way*. We wanted God to pull us by the hand into his perfect will, but all we had was the gentle nudge of peace.

A few years into our marriage, those insecure decisions turned into firm footing. We found a church that introduced us to our future ministries. BJ went on to excel in his career path. I found a teaching opportunity within walking distance of our residence. That tiny apartment became a launching pad for our first couples' Bible Study. One of the members of that group became a lifelong friend and staff member for the non-profit organization I operate today. Sometimes I felt like God winked at me with an *I told you so*. All my worries were pointless. The Lord knew these details from the start.

God desires his will for your life more than you do. Fear of missing his plans is unnecessary when your heart is following him. Some psychologists say that decision-making is the primary cause of anxiety in millennials. A spiritual momma once told me, "When you don't know what to do, follow peace." She would then quote Colossians, "And let the peace that comes from Christ rule in your hearts" (Colossians 3:15 NLT). *Rule* in Greek means "to umpire." Let the peace of God call the shots. Allow the Holy Spirit to shape your thoughts so that you recognize his will.

One day as I scanned Scripture, a familiar verse caught my attention in a new light. "Don't copy the behavior and customs of this world, but let God transform you into a new person by changing the way you think. Then you will learn to know God's will for you, which is good and pleasing and perfect" (Romans 12:2 NLT). I highlighted the verse. I noticed another translation said it differently: "Be transformed by the renewing of your mind" (NKJV). The renewed mind readily recognizes the will of God. My mental state is a mess when I haven't been with the Father. Worries try to wrestle down my faith. As I seek the Lord in prayer, my thoughts are transformed. God's will becomes recognizable.

As I think about my prayer time, I am reminded of how the Bible describes Moses' relationship with God. "The LORD would speak to Moses face to face, as one speaks to a friend" (Exodus 33:11 NLT). When friends spend time together, it's easy to pick up on facial expressions. When we are with God, we may not see his physical face, yet his presence carries the expression of his nature. We learn his ways through Scripture. God's thoughts shape our thoughts. A line from the apostle Paul puts it this way: "Put on your new nature, and be renewed as you learn to know your Creator and become like him" (Colossians 3:10 NLT). You may be thinking, *how do we know when our minds are renewed?* Bill Johnson explains it this way: "When the impossible looks logical."[55]

You can rest knowing that the Father takes the lead as you trust him. His plans may not always be easy, but they are filled with peace. Remember that he will never abandon you (Deuteronomy 31:6–8). God's will is always good, and he never fails.

Pause to Reflect

- When you are not sure what to do, follow peace.
- If you want to know God's plans for your life, allow him to transform your thoughts.
- The mind is renewed through daily interaction with God.

Pause to Pray

Lord, I want your purposes for my life. I surrender my will to yours. As I spend time with you, transform my thinking. Lead me forward on your path as I trust you. In Jesus' name I pray. Amen.

Dream Seeds

"This vision is for a future time.
It describes the end, and it will be fulfilled.
If it seems slow in coming, wait patiently,
for it will surely take place."
HABAKKUK 2:3 NLT

I imagined Joseph in the prison washroom staring into a broken mirror. Hardship had faded the face of the young man he once saw. He prayed, *What did I do to mess up my calling, Lord? I thought I was so special. Well, look at me now, a prisoner to Egyptian pagans.* There was little time to clean up before being rushed to Pharaoh's court, but Joseph couldn't help his mind from wandering.

His thoughts flashed to when he was seventeen. He had woken up wide-eyed from a dream that God had given him the night before. Images had flashed in his mind of his family bowing to him in reverence. After the vision, it made sense that his father had given him a special robe. Joseph ran his fingers along the ornate hem. The coat was *fit for royalty*, his father had said. Joseph slid the robe over his shoulders and tied the waist. He took one last look in the hand mirror, then burst out the door to ramble to his brothers about the dream.

Back in the prison washroom, Joseph rinsed his cleanly shaven face and head. His mind drifted forward to his fate. Why was he being summoned to Pharaoh? Joseph remembered the cupbearer and baker that were imprisoned with him two years ago. The cupbearer was later restored to his place of prominence while the baker was impaled on a pole. Which would be Joseph's destiny? Joseph put on the clean clothes provided by the jailer. He thought about how God had been with him on his journey. Whatever would happen today, he would be in the Lord's hands.

At first glance, Joseph's story seems more tragic than triumphant. He was his father's favorite son, and his God-given dreams enraged his brothers. Motivated by jealousy, the brothers sold Joseph to slave traders. He ended up as a servant to Potiphar, an Egyptian palace guard officer. Although Joseph was a slave, God promoted him as overseer to Potiphar's house. When Joseph refused the sexual advances of Potiphar's wife, she reported attempted rape. Imprisonment seemed to be Joseph's outcome for obeying God. The Lord granted Joseph favor in the prison, positioning him as second in command behind the warden. Although he was favored, Joseph still wasn't free. Thirteen years passed since he had received his dreams, and surely, they seemed lost at the bottom of the dungeon.

God promoted Joseph from the prison to the palace in one moment. Joseph's years of preparation collided in one conversation. Pharaoh had summoned him because he heard that Joseph could interpret dreams. Pharaoh had two night visions that the royal magicians could not decipher. God led Joseph to predict that the dreams symbolized seven years of prosperity followed by seven years of famine. Joseph spoke up with wisdom to help Pharaoh prepare for scarcity in the nation. Pharaoh was so impressed that he promoted Joseph to second in command of the kingdom, or vizier, over all Egypt. Palace servants draped elaborate jewelry and fine clothes over Joseph.

Part of his role as vizier meant that Joseph handled all foreign relations. Years later, a group of Jewish shepherds, Joseph's brothers, arrived in Egypt seeking aid during the famine. Soldiers sent the shepherds to the vizier. Joseph's brothers, and eventually his parents, bowed before him in respect. Joseph saved millions of people with the wisdom he gained in servitude. After twenty years, God fulfilled the visions he planted in Joseph's heart.

Don't fear that your dreams are dead when trapped in a dungeon season. Dormant seeds sprout in the dark. There is often preparation picked up in troubled times. I encourage you to learn what you can through the challenges. Ask God to prepare the soil of your heart so the dream-seeds can be sustained. When the time is right, those dreams will bear fruit and impact generations following behind you.

Pause to Reflect

- God does not revoke our gifts and callings.
- The condition of our hearts needs to be soft to support the dreams within us.
- Although the dream seeds may look dead in difficult times, challenges are often what make them grow.

Pause to Pray

Lord, you know the plans you have for me. They are always for my good and not for disaster. Help me cling to you in times of trouble. Grow the dreams you planted within me. In Jesus' name I pray. Amen.

Get Up and Run

Therefore, since we are surrounded by such a huge crowd of witnesses to the life of faith, let us strip off every weight that slows us down, especially the sin that so easily trips us up. And let us run with endurance the race God has set before us. We do this by keeping our eyes on Jesus, the champion who initiates and perfects our faith.

HEBREWS 12:1–2 NLT

The runner was sprawled flat on the track as her competitors sprinted by. The roar of the stadium fell silent. The shoo-in for the 600-meter race had most likely just lost the championship. A flat-fall was a death sentence in a three-lap race.

Heather Dorniden was no ordinary athlete. After falling hard to the ground, she gave a solid shove on the track, righted herself, and took off in pursuit of the runners. Most of the audience counted her out. Knowing that her team needed to score points, Heather pushed harder than she had before. She quickly closed the gap between her and the fourth-place runner. She sprinted past the competitor at the rear of the pack. The announcers were in shock, "This is a gutsy effort by Dorniden. Can she pull it off?" The third runner was no match for Heather. She willed herself forward. As the group rounded the last corner, she pressed past the second-place sprinter. One last push would decide the race as Dorniden pushed for first.

With the finish line in sight, she gave fearless effort. The announcers breathlessly called, "Dorniden coming down the stretch from the outside!" The entire stadium jumped to their feet. "Dorniden coming on strong!" As they sprinted down the last straightaway, she matched the first-place runner stride for stride. They pushed toward the line. "Dorniden all the way!" Heather and her competitor lunged toward the finish line neck and neck. "She did it!" Her coach leaped in the air and hugged the teammates on the side-lines. Heather Dorniden secured the championship and made history as one of the few runners who fell during a race and still finished first.[56]

The race of life isn't always easy. There are mis-steps, hurdles, and bruises along the way. We entangle with setbacks and inevitably stumble. Sometimes we trip over other runners, and often we falter over our own two feet. When we fall, we're faced with a choice: Do we crumple in defeat or push back in defiance?

We can choose to view failure as finality or fuel for the next lap. At times we may feel like we're running alone. Often the track feels long, and we lose stamina. Then there are days when our steps become laborious as our feet feel weighted with bricks.

When I was younger and in better shape, I ran with my mom's old ankle weights. I strapped the bright blue bags around my ankles and jogged through our neighborhood. Then I would reach down, unstrap the Velcro, and toss the weights to the side. I can still feel the freedom of those weights coming off. My heavy jog felt effortless as I bounded down the road. Running was easier when there was less resistance.

Shackles of shame, fear, and condemnation, among others, often hold us back from running at full speed. Carrying these burdens can cause unnecessary fatigue and injury. While these weights make our gait heavy, they also cause us to fix our eyes on dangerous places. Looking straight down in shame, backward in condemnation, or all-around in fear may cause us to trip and fall. Scripture calls us to focus on Jesus, the champion of our faith. He carried our sorrows to the cross. As we stride with him, he sets the momentum at the pace of grace. No longer striving under a heavy load, we have the freedom to run with endurance.

Let Jesus unstrap any weights you wear today. Your frame was not designed to carry their burdens.

Be the prize runner who reflects the image of the Creator. Shake off the shackles and run light. You are a champion because Jesus lives in you.

Pause to Reflect

- The race of life often comes with bumps, holes, and hurdles.
- On the cross, Jesus took the weights of sin and sorrow.
- When we remove restraints, we run with stamina and joy.

Pause to Pray

Lord Jesus, I want to run my race well. I ask you to lift off all weights from my shoulders. I confess my sins to you. Please forgive and cleanse me. I don't have to live with the heaviness of guilt, shame, and fear. Take them away, Lord. Heal me and help me run with you at the pace of grace. In Jesus' name I pray. Amen.

Crafting Art

For we are God's masterpiece. He has created us anew in Christ Jesus, so we can do the good things he planned for us long ago.
EPHESIANS 2:10 NLT

One of the largest sapphires in history sat as a doorstop for nine years in Queensland, Australia. A twelve-year-old boy plucked it out of a pile of rubble in 1938. His father used the heavy rock to prop open the door of his old mining shack. One day, a world-renowned gemologist visited the area sourcing jewels for his business. The black rock caught his eye as he entered the family's home. He turned it over in his experienced hands running his fingers around the curves and colors. The gemologist was elated at possibly discovering the world's largest star sapphire. He purchased the stone for $18,000, or about $196,000 in today's economy.[57]

Back in his lab, the gemologist studied the rock for months before cutting it. One wrong move could demolish the precious gem. Once the cutting was complete, the Black Star of Queensland resulted in a 733-carat star sapphire. This rare optical formation produced a six-point golden shape in the center of the gem. The star within the sapphire was the most pronounced when exposed to rays of light.[58] Today the stone is worth $88 million,[59] has toured museums worldwide, and has adorned famous movie stars.[60] A rare jewel was hidden within the rock, but it required the right eyes to see it.

Ordinary is a label we pin on people far too quickly. We rub shoulders with neighbors, coworkers, and acquaintances and miss the extraordinary gifts hidden within them. Interestingly, perhaps the person we misjudge the most is ourselves. We criticize, condemn, and conceal precious gems tucked within our hearts.

Average may seem like your name lately. You might feel hidden in obscurity or like people are blind to your value. Remember that Jesus thought so highly of you that he paid the costly price of the cross for your life. Allow God's gentle hands to uncover your hidden worth. Surrender to the correction of the Holy Spirit as he breaks away pieces that would bury your potential. Yield to his careful nudges of instruction as he crafts your calling. Like a sapphire, the light of God will cause the secret star within you to shine brightly.

In the Old Testament, God uncovered the value of a king concealed in a kid when he called David from the sheep field. The fifteen-year-old son of Jesse seemed forgotten by his family. The prophet Samuel came to Bethlehem and called a sacrificial feast. God had sent Samuel to anoint the next king from the sons of Jesse. However, Jesse did not invite David. The prophet took one look at Eliab, the oldest brother, and thought, *Surely this must be the next king!* God corrected Samuel, "The LORD doesn't see things the way you see them. People judge by outward appearance, but the LORD looks at the heart" (1 Samuel 16:7 NLT). This response applied to the rest of Jesse's seven older sons. They all matched people's perception of royalty, but God had another plan.

Exasperated, Samuel asked, "Don't you have any more sons?"

Jesse almost ignored the request, "Yeah, there's one more, but he's out tending sheep."

Samuel demanded, "Go get him at once." David was handsome, but surely, he was smaller than expected for a king. God saw something in David that others could not. He spoke to Samuel, "This is the one; anoint him" (v. 12). The family saw a shepherd, but the Lord saw a warrior.

David became one of the most beloved people in biblical history. He conquered giants, slayed enemies, and promoted peace as king of Israel. David's forty-year reign brought great prosperity to the nation. He wasn't a man without faults, but he found favor with God. Jesus Christ was among those in David's lineage, and his star is displayed on Israel's flag today.

God placed priceless potential inside you. There are intricacies of your design that remain undiscovered. Next time you look in the mirror, remember that you are a masterpiece in the making by a creative God.

Pause to Reflect

- The image of God shines within you.
- Your design is not defective.
- God's love flowing through you reveals your value to the world.

Pause to Pray

Father, when I feel unseen and unwanted, you know my name. Uncover my potential. Please show me how special I am to you. Shape me into the artwork you created me to be. In Jesus' name I pray. Amen.

Acknowledgments

To my love, BJ Ward. You are my hero every day and support when life is heavy. I am beyond proud to be your wife.

Thank you to our beautiful kids, Abbey, Emma, and Evan. God knows how much you gave to see this work come to pass. Remember that the rewards from those reading it belong to you too.

Thank you to my parents, Kim and Steve Fults and Gary and Rhonda Rayborn, for all your sacrifices. I am who I am because of you and Jesus.

To Bishop Jimmy and Pastor Karen Davidson, my ministry looks like yours because of what you've instilled in me. You have my utmost gratitude, love, and respect. *With my whole heart* for life!

Thank you, Dr. Tracey Mitchell, for believing in my calling and, at times, pulling out my gifts. You were a godsend at the right time. I honor your wise experience and sacrificial heart.

Grace to Grow team, the best is yet to come. Thank you for your dedication, prayers, and support. You make the magic happen every week. I'm honored to serve with you.

Thank you to my loving and loyal family and friends. You make me better every day. I'm grateful that I get to do life with you.

To my Lord, where would I be without you? All of this is for you and because of you. I pray that I followed you closely, released your words, and spoke with your heart. Thank you for such a beautiful journey.

About Kristel Ward

Kristel Ward is an insightful Bible teacher and inspiring conference speaker. With a background in public education and pastoral ministry, her biblical wisdom has encouraged thousands to follow the example of Christ.

In 2016, Kristel's life came to a sudden halt when her four-month-old son had a critical reaction to medication. Over thirty days, he suffered more than seventy seizures. The mental and emotional trauma of not knowing if her son would live, die, or have a quality of life forced Kristel to dig deep into her spiritual roots. She emerged from that season with a stronger understanding of the Bible and an unquenchable passion to share it.

By combining her communication, ministry, and education skills, Kristel launched a nonprofit organization, Grace to Grow. Each week Kristel leads a team of ministers to spiritually and emotionally support women around the globe. Whether from behind the podium, social media platforms, or camera productions, Kristel helps busy people grow in their relationship with God.

Kristel is married to BJ Ward. Together they have three beautiful, smart, and sometimes messy children, Abbey, Emma, and Evan. The Ward family enjoys road trips, the outdoors, and a good campfire.

Connect with Kristel on her website (kristelward.com), Facebook (@kristelwardtx), Instagram (@kristel_wardtx), and TikTok (@kristelwardtx).

Endnotes

1   *Fireproof*, directed by Alex Kendrick (2008; Albany, GA: Sherwood Pictures, 2009), DVD, 122 minutes.

2   Timothy Yap, "Story behind Darlene Zschech's 'Shout to the Lord,'" Jubilee Cast, April 1, 2016, http://www.hallels.com/articles/15075/20160401/story-behind-darlene-zschechs-shout-to-the-lord.htm.

3   Yap, "Zschech's 'Shout to the Lord.'"

4   Coach Aaron, "The Art of Counter Punching," Commando Boxing, January 13, 2018, https://commandoboxing.com/the-art-of-counter-punching.

5   "Philly Shell," Boxing Undefeated, accessed December 8, 2021, https://boxingundefeated.com/defense/guards/philly-shell/.

6   Jerry Bridges, *Transforming Grace* (Carol Stream, IL: NavPress, 1991), 134. Used by permission of NavPress, www.navpress.com. All rights reserved.

7   *A Good Year*, directed by Ridley Scott (2006, Los Angeles: 20th Century Fox, 2007), DVD, 118 minutes.

8   Robert Graves, *Goodbye to All That* (New York: Penguin, 1965), 35.

9   "Did Mallory Make It?" *National Geographic* (website), accessed on November 5, 2021, https://www.nationalgeographic.org/media/did-mallory-make-it-9-12/.

10 Liesl Clark and Audrey Salkeld, "The Mystery of Mallory and Irvine '24," NOVA Online Adventure, WGBH PBS, November 2000, https://www.pbs.org/wgbh/nova/everest/lost/mystery/.

11 Callum Hoare, "Mount Everest Mystery Solved? Mallory's Oxygen Tank 'Broken' before Summit Climb," *Express, Daily Express*, November 6, 2019, https://www.express.co.uk/news/world/1200299/mount-everest-mystery-george-mallory-andrew-irwine-oxygen-bottle-broken-spt.

12 Hoare, "Mount Everest Mystery Solved?"

13 Jon Excell, "June 1953: Oxygen Breathing Kit for Climbers on Mount Everest," *The Engineer*, June 8, 2017, https://www.theengineer.co.uk/june-1953-oxygen-breathing-kit-for-climbers-on-mount-everest/.

14 Excell, "June 1953: Oxygen Breathing Kit."

15 "Did Mallory Make It?"

16 "Did Mallory Make It?"

17 Missy Robinson, "When He Leaves," Far from Flawless (blog), January 24, 2011, http://farfromflawlesslife.blogspot.com/2011/01/when-he-leaves.html.

18 Lisa Fritscher, "Understanding Fear of Abandonment," VeryWell Mind, June 15, 2020, https://www.verywellmind.com/fear-of-abandonment-2671741.

19 "Coping with Loss: Grief Data and Stats You Need to Know," Eterneva, accessed on November 5, 2021, https://eterneva.com/resources/coping-with-loss.

20 "Abandonment," GoodTherapy, last modified on November 21, 2019, https://www.goodtherapy.org/learn-about-therapy/issues/abandonment.

21 A. W. Tozer, "The Winsome Saints," YouVersion, accessed January 12, 2022, https://www.bible.com/ reading-plans/16810-7-mornings-with-aw-tozer/ day/5.

22 "Gender and Stress," American Psychological Association, accessed on November 5, 2021, https://www.apa.org/news/press/releases/ stress/2010/gender-stress.

23 "Where Americans Find Meaning in Life," Pew Research Center, November 20, 2018, https://www.pewforum.org/2018/11/20/ where-americans-find-meaning-in-life/.

24 *Friends*, season 8, episode 9, "The One with the Rumor," directed by Gary Halvorson, aired November 22, 2001, on NBC.

25 Katherine Hassell, "Friends like These: Fun Facts about the 20-Year-Old Sitcom," *Express, Daily Express*, September 14, 2014, https:// www.express.co.uk/showbiz/tv-radio/509982/ Fun-Friends-facts.

26 Brendan Morrow, "The Most Watched TV Series Finales of All Time," *Showbiz Cheat Sheet*, July 10, 2018, https://www.cheatsheet.com/entertainment/ the-most-watched-tv-series-finales-of-all-time. html/.

27 "Loneliness in America: How the Pandemic Has Deepened an Epidemic of Loneliness and What We Can Do about It," Making Caring Common Project, Harvard Graduate School of Education, February 2021, https://mcc.gse.harvard.edu/reports/loneliness-in-america.

28 Zoya Gervis, "Why the Average American Hasn't Made a New Friend in 5 Years," *New York Post*, May 9, 2019, https://nypost.com/2019/05/09/why-the-average-american-hasnt-made-a-new-friend-in-5-years/.

29 Gervis, "Why the Average American Hasn't Made a New Friend."

30 Gervis, "Why the Average American Hasn't Made a New Friend."

31 Joseph Burgo, "The Health Benefits of Friendship," Fix, March 9, 2015, https://www.fix.com/blog/health-benefits-of-friendship/.

32 *John Q.*, directed by Nick Cassavetes (2002, Los Angeles: Evolution Entertainment, 2002), DVD, 116 minutes.

33 "Identifying Emotional Triggers: Common Triggers and What They Mean," Port St. Lucie Hospital, May 7, 2021, https://www.portstluciehospitalinc.com/identifying-emotional-triggers-common-triggers-what-they-mean/.

34 Crystal Raypole, "How to Identify and Manage Your Emotional Triggers," Healthline, November 13, 2020, https://www.healthline.com/health/mental-health/emotional-triggers#finding-yours.

35 Raypole, "How to Identify and Manage Your Emotional Triggers."

36 Adapted from Mark 4:1–9 (NLT).

37 Corrie ten Boom, *Common Sense Not Needed: Bringing the Gospel to the Developmentally Disabled* (Fort Washington, PA: CLC Publications, 2012), chap. 3.

38 Adapted from John 4:4–30 (NIV).

39 *The Oprah Winfrey Show*, season 23, episode 61, "David Blaine Breaks a World Record for Holding His Breath under Water," directed by Joseph C. Terry, aired April 30, 2008, on ABC, https://www.oprah.com/own-oprahshow/david-blaine-breaks-a-world-record-for-holding-his-breath-under-water.

40 Alex Hutchinson, "How Does Your Brain Respond When You Hold Your Breath?" *Outside*, Outside Interactive, Inc., November 25, 2020, https://www.outsideonline.com/health/training-performance/breath-holding-research-2020/.

41 Lynne Eldridge, "Hypoxia: Types and Overview," VeryWell Health, November 19, 2020, https://www.verywellhealth.com/hypoxia-types-symptoms-and-causes-2248929.

42 Charles R. Swindoll, *Wisdom for the Way: Wise Words for Busy People* (Nashville, TN: Thomas Nelson, 2007), 143.

43 Kritter Klub, "Bald Eagle Fond of Walking, Thinks Hunting Is Too Savage," YouTube, November 27, 2019, https://www.youtube.com/watch?v=gsO7lmS8XG8.

44 Pauline Rose Clance, "Imposter Phenomenon (IP)," Pauline Rose Clance, Atlanta Psychologist (website), accessed on November 5, 2021, https://paulineroseclance.com/impostor_phenomenon.html.

45 Clance, "Imposter Phenomenon."

46 Olivia Fox Cabane, "Do You Suffer from Imposter Syndrome?" *HuffPost*, May 23, 2012, https://www.huffpost.com/entry/self-doubt_b_1373542.

47 Laura Johnson, "Imposter Syndrome: Are You Discounting Yourself and Your Successes?" Cognitive Behavior Therapy Center, accessed on November 5, 2021, http://cognitivebehaviortherapycenter.com/impostor-syndrome/.

48 Andy Molinsky, "Everyone Suffers from Imposter Syndrome: Here's How to Handle It," Harvard Business Review, July 7, 2016, https://hbr.org/2016/07/everyone-suffers-from-imposter-syndrome-heres-how-to-handle-it.

49 R. Kress, "Paralyzed by Self-Doubt? 3 Tips for Overcoming 'Imposter Syndrome,'" Ivy Exec, accessed on November 5, 2021, https://www.ivyexec.com/career-advice/2017/overcoming-imposter-syndrome-tips/.

50 Megan Dalia-Camina, "The Reality of Imposter Syndrome," *Psychology Today*, September 3, 2018, https://www.psychologytoday.com/us/blog/real-women/201809/the-reality-imposter-syndrome.

51 *Frozen*, directed by Chris Buck and Jennifer Lee (2013, Burbank, CA: Walt Disney Pictures, 2014), DVD, 102 minutes.

52 Adapted from 2 Kings 4: 1–7 (NLT).

53 Havilah Cunnington, *Eat. Pray. Hustle.: Dream Chasing God's Way* (self-pub., 2015), 60.

54 *This Is Us*, season 2, episode 14, "Super Bowl Sunday," directed by Glenn Ficarra and John Requa, aired on February 4, 2018, on NBC, 46 minutes.

55 Bill Johnson, "The Supernatural Power of a Transformed Mind," Bill Johnson Ministries, accessed on November 5, 2021, https://bjm.org/core-values/the-supernatural-power-of-a-transformed-mind/.

56 "Heather Dorniden Wins the Race," 2008 Big Ten Indoor Track Championships, YouTube, posted August 29, 2020, https://www.youtube.com/watch?v=g9rUUz8cMDM.

57 "World's Largest Gem-Quality Star Sapphire Served as a Dusty Doorstop for Nine Years," The Jeweler Blog, September 2, 2015, https://thejewelerblog.wordpress.com/2015/09/02/worlds-largest-gem-quality-star-sapphire-served-as-a-dusty-doorstop-for-nine-years/.

58 Shihaan Larif, "The Black Star of Queensland Famous Black Sapphire Gemstone," Internet Stones Media, February 19, 2008, https://news.internetstones.com/the-black-star-of-queensland-famous-black-sapphire-gemstone/.

59 Larif, "The Black Star of Queensland."

60 "World's Largest Gem-Quality Star Sapphire Served as a Dusty Doorstop."